Communicating with Your Staff

Also in the Orion Business Toolkit Series

Communicating with Your Staff

Patrick Forsyth

ORION
BUSINESS
BOOKS

First published in Great Britain in 1999 by
Orion Business

An imprint of The Orion Publishing Group Ltd
Orion House, 5 Upper St Martin's Lane, London WC2H 9EA

A CIP catalogue record for this book
is available from the British Library

ISBN 0-75283-090-2

Typeset by Deltatype Ltd, Birkenhead, Merseyside
Printed and bound by
Guernsey Press, C.I.

For Jacqui – managing already.

I think that the fundamental process of conversation is one of the great miracles of nature, that two people communicating with each other is an extraordinary phenomenon that has so far defied all attempts to capture it. There have been attempts made in many different disciplines – in cognitive science, in linguistics, in social theory – and no one has really made much progress. Communicating with another person remains an essentially mystical act.

Jaron Lanier

Contents

Introduction

There is no magic in management. I make sure that people know what they are doing and then see that they do it.

(Bob Scholey)

Management is easy. It consists of little more than sitting in an ivory tower, issuing instructions and keeping an eye open to see if people need chasing to be sure they are executing them properly. Or so it may seem. Of course management is, in fact, no easy task and it can prove downright difficult, especially if the overall business or corporate climate in which it is practised is less than ideal.

A simple definition will help to set the scene. Management describes the process of achieving results *through* other people. It is different from doing things *for* them, and it is inherent to the process that management should add to what others would otherwise do of their own volition – or there might be considered to be little point in having managers at all. Managers, of course, often have their own tasks to complete alongside the job of managing others. Yet managing other people is usually crucial; however productive and creative a manager may be, they can never, through their own efforts, make up for ineffective performance amongst their team. Thus the job of being a manager must be carried out effectively if overall results are to be achieved successfully, and this in turn involves many different tasks.

➡ THE MANAGEMENT PORTFOLIO

Managers have many things to do to set up and maintain an

effective team. The process involves six key activities:

- recruitment and selection
- organising the team
- planning the activities of the group (whether a department or a whole organisation)
- developing people so that they can, and can continue to be able to, perform effectively
- motivating people so that they want to perform
- executing appropriate control of what is done (and initiating revised plans along the way if necessary).

In undertaking these tasks, a manager will be involved in a host of subsidiary processes and must have skills to execute them all effectively. Such may include: interviewing; managing meetings; briefing, training and appraising staff; making presentations; writing reports; and much more. Management also needs to include less formal tasks and characteristics: from patience to persistence, and from being a shoulder to cry on to being a leader to follow. In addition, it may involve skills such as numeracy and computer literacy and whatever technical skills the work of a particular organisation necessitates. And there really are people who say management is easy!

➡ A COMMON THREAD

Leaving specialist skills on one side for the moment – but only because what they are may vary from manager to manager somewhat – we can consider what it is that links so many aspects of the management job. The common thread is, in a word, communication. Almost everything one might list in the same breath as the word 'management' involves, or is a form of, communication. The implication is clear: to be a good manager, someone must be a good communicator. *If you cannot communicate clearly, you cannot manage effectively.*

Not all managers are good communicators, of course. Some may admit it, but 'muddle through somehow', perhaps feeling other characteristics are more important or make up for shortfalls in communication. Perhaps an alternative, and a positively expressed, maxim is a better starting point for a book such as this:

Good communication can make management success more certain and more likely to achieve excellence.

This is the theme of this book. It is not the book's task to give a review of all the skills that the management process involves, nor to investigate deeply the technical factors that they may, necessarily, need to incorporate. For example, in dealing with people, such topics as employment legislation or unionisation may occasionally be important and may be mentioned here, but the book does not set out to cover such matters in detail. This is not to negate the importance of such subjects, but the intention is to follow the common theme, focus on the specific part that communication plays within the management process, and review in what ways *what* is done and *how* it is done can help the process.

➡ THE INTENDED READER

This book is written with two groups of readership in mind.

First, it is aimed primarily at first-line managers, i.e. those who manage a team and have others reporting to them. Because good communication does not occur spontaneously and is not everyone's inherent stock in trade, the target reader in this group may be a new or a more experienced manager. The objectives here are clear, namely to:

- show the necessity for clear, appropriate communication between managers and staff, particularly in the business climate that is current and foreseen as we enter the new millennium
- illustrate the opportunities involved, i.e. show how good communications can contribute to the achievement of whatever results are planned
- review 'how-to' elements about the kind of communications involved in management and see how effectiveness can be maximised.

Second, it is hoped that this book will be of value in a broader sense and help those interested in improving communications around their organisation rather than (or as well as) improving their own. Certainly, broader implications are referred to as the chapters unfold.

It is a firm intention that the book should be useful whatever the nature of the people reporting to you. Some will readily be described as subordinates, others will be near equals and others still will in effect be largely independent agents, as with senior professional staff in, say, an accountancy practice – and such people, however specialised and expert, may well still need managing.

➡ THE SPECIAL INGREDIENT

Most economies around the world have been through difficult, or at least different and unpredictable, times in recent years; indeed, 'getting back to normal' does not seem an option for which it is worth waiting. It is axiomatic that managers bear the brunt of any commercial or organisational challenge. They must cope with declining markets, ever more fickle customers, financial and corporate upheaval and a more dynamic business environment than has ever existed in the past. The IT (information technology) revolution, to take one example, is evidence enough of the rate of change that managers must contend with daily. It is not just doom and gloom that creates problems. Positive developments too – for example, as a company launches a new product onto a growing market – are equally likely to give managers and their team challenging tasks. Of course success, when it is achieved, is influenced by many things. Some, such as sheer hard work or persistence, are likely to be as important as more technical or innovative ones.

But when push comes to shove, it is people who create success. And managers have the job of leading and supervising their people. Take people out of the organisation and there is little, if anything, left. Similarly, take the communication out of management and management ceases to exist in any meaningful way. If management makes a difference, then communications excellence throughout the process makes a difference to management and what management can achieve. It may not be a real magic formula (if only a real one existed!), but attention to it can certainly produce improved results.

Chapter 1
Maximising staff effectiveness

You impress folks that little bit more with what you're saying if you say it nicely. People don't hear your ideas if you just stand there shouting out words.

(Lord Gormley)

The management job varies. It encompasses those who maintain a situation, who keep a department or section not simply ticking over but performing efficiently and productively, but perhaps with no pressing need to develop or innovate. It also includes those whose job is inherently better described as concerned with the initiation of things, with innovation, change and creativity. Whatever part of the continuum between these two extremes is involved – and it should be said that coping with or initiating change affects more and more managers nowadays – any manager is dependent on his or her team. That could be a secretary and an assistant, a department of 20 people or a whole organisation. Now, make no mistake: management is a big job. As the tasks and characteristics listed in the Introduction make clear, there is a good deal to do – and none of it just happens. *To be effective, the process of management needs consideration, time and effort.*

Good communication cannot change this fact, but it can increase the chances of effectiveness of what is being done. The best managers treat their team like royalty, the most important people in their working lives. The best managers work at helping the team succeed.

In simple terms and assuming they have the ability to do the job, what is required is the creation of a team who work:

- efficiently
- effectively

- reliably
- consistently
- productively.

Ideally, it is also necessary for people to be focused on the job and to have an appropriate degree of self-sufficiency (to be 'empowered' was the expression in vogue for a while) so that the manager can manage from a distance. If good performance is only achieved by watching people every step of the way, this is time-consuming and hardly reflects an effective team performance. A good team is quick on its feet – and that too is a characteristic brought out by good management.

➡ THE ROLE OF COMMUNICATIONS

Communication is inherent to the management process. Whether a manager wants to prompt a specific action, instigate discussion or idea generation, change attitudes, or go through specific communications processes such as staff appraisal, it all starts with communication – and good communication can ensure or enhance all these processes. But it may stop there too. So first let us consider the problems that poor communication can create.

Negative effects

The ways in which poor, or ill-judged, communication might have a negative impact are legion. The evidence of poor communication is all around us in most (perhaps all) organisations. Walk through the typical office and you will hear the likes of the following floating in the air: 'I thought you meant . . .', 'But you said to . . .', 'No, what I meant to say was . . .', 'Why didn't you say that in the first place?'

Sometimes such conversations do no great harm – at least not beyond a momentary hiatus while something is sorted out through an explanatory phrase or two. On other occasions more harm is done: incorrect action is taken, time is wasted, money is spent unnecessarily, and deadlines are missed. The effect can be external too, possibly resulting in upset or inconvenienced customers who may even take their business elsewhere. There is a dilution of effectiveness at work here, the dangers of which will be readily clear (and we look at exactly why this sort of thing happens and how to avoid it in Chapter 3).

All this may come from a brief, but ill-thought-out few words of conversation. Or much more time and effort may be involved. Someone might, for example, spend hours writing a long, detailed report only to find that it was unnecessary because the initial instruction had meant something else. This is something that is not just an example of waste and inefficiency but that can be personally demoralising to those involved as well. Consider some examples before moving on:

- *Recruitment and selection* can be a chore. It is, however, a vital task because having the right people in place is a differentiating factor for any organisation. Yet a single ill-prepared interview, with maybe just a few questions asked in the wrong way (or not asked at all) and the result – the right candidate missed or the wrong one appointed – may produce consequences for the organisation that must be lived with for a considerable time.

- *Appraisal* is another major interviewing task with similar potential for problems. Again, such a meeting is not the easiest thing to conduct, and if communications break down then maybe an employee who should have been nurtured for the future benefit of the firm is found to be leaving in six months' time.

- *Time off*. Here is something much smaller in scale, where (for instance) a member of staff asks for time off for good reason but pressure of the moment and looking ahead prompts a manager to give an offhand, negative answer. Staff motivation – as well as productivity – can sometimes be easily affected and take time to repair.

The desirability of avoiding such instances, large or small, will be clear. But the reverse of all this is perhaps where the focus must lie. It is not enough to avoid breakdowns in communication and get the communication right; it is important to get the most from the situation by executing the communication as well as possible.

Positive impact

The clarity of a message clearly has an effect on what occurs next. Potential problems have already been hinted at: poor communication at best produces confusion; at worst it fails to help achieve whatever should be achieved. Conversely, ensuring that a message is clear and unambiguous can result in positive action. Exactly what should get done gets done. Such communication is directly able to:

- speed up action
- improve efficiency
- increase productivity
- stimulate creativity.

Indeed, it will act as a spur to whatever action is required. This may literally be an action, for some management communication is in the nature of an instruction; but it may also be designed for other purposes, for instance to:

- inform
- instruct
- motivate
- change opinions
- prompt debate or discussion
- stimulate the generation of ideas
- build on prior contacts or thinking.

Such a list could doubtless be extended and makes two points: that there is a great deal hanging on any communication between management and staff; and that it is worth getting it right if your intentions as a manager are to be achieved as you wish.

Chapter 3 investigates something of the psychology involved in communication: what causes communications breakdowns and what helps prevent them. Here are some examples:

- *Instruction*. There is all the difference between asking someone 'to get some information out immediately' (what is 'immediately' exactly?) and saying that it must go to someone 'by fax, before three o'clock this afternoon'. The latter sort of precision is one of the ways in which an appropriate outcome can be assured. Other examples exemplify further. The following choose topics other than those mentioned in a negative light above (although each has their positive side).

- *Training* can be very valuable (and I say this not just because I undertake training work!), but this is not always the case. A briefing meeting where time is skimped and needs are wrongly identified can result in a member of staff attending a course that is neither enjoyable nor beneficial, and that sours the individual's view of training for the future. In contrast, good pre-course (and post-course, for that matter) communication can enhance the training experience, changing a planned course attendance from something viewed as an awkward break in other work to something that is looked forward to, worked at open-mindedly and from which someone draws real benefit.

- *Incentives* are designed to prompt additional effort and make targeted results more likely to be achieved. Incentive schemes are not universal panaceas, but they can be very worthwhile in the right context. And yet more than one such scheme has failed because managers have failed to listen to their staff, and the managers end up instigating a scheme with no appeal to the people it is intended to influence. (Indeed, sometimes perhaps the incentive rewards are picked solely because they appeal to the manager!). Discussion beforehand can help devise an appropriate scheme, and clear communication of the whys and wherefores of it can ensure it hits the spot and works well.

- *Rumour and bad news* is a danger area. 'Leave it alone and it will go away' is sometimes the most tempting attitude to adopt, more because dealing with it is awkward rather than because of a real belief that that course of action will work. However, clear, positive communication powerfully put over at the right time can stop a rumour dead in its tracks and get motivation heading in the right direction again.

The bonus of message plus method

Communication involves three elements: the message, the delivery method used, and the messenger. All are important. The clarity (or otherwise) of any message has an obvious effect on the results it is intended to achieve. But the message alone is not the sole influence; the method of communication matters too.

There are things that are best done at a meeting; in a letter, memo, fax or e-mail; or by one-to-one conversation on the telephone or in a moment as two people pass in a corridor. Yet each method is as unsuitable for some things as it is right for others. Few would appreciate being fired by e-mail. The same could be said of the reverse: being promoted surely deserves some discussion, a formal letter of appointment and a sense of occasion. And combinations of media can be used: in our example, a promotion might be discussed in person, confirmation sent by fax (to delay the good news not at all), discussion might then again follow, and then written confirmation – a letter or memo – to complete and confirm the detail.

In every circumstance, one of the things that deserves thought is the choice of method. This means a concentration on the recipient and the result. It may be quicker and easier just to lift a telephone, but other ways may have more lasting impact and power. Consider how much stronger the effect is of receiving a thank-you letter compared with a quick telephone call. Of course, each method has its place, and each is best for some applications and less good for others.

The third element mentioned above is the messenger. What can the individual bring to bear on all this? Some ideas on this topic are set out in the next section.

➡ THE POWER OF POSITIVE IMAGE

The view that people hold of an individual manager will also have an impact on the way that manager's communications are regarded and acted upon. The factors affecting how a manager is regarded, by immediate staff and others, are not easy to tie down for there are many such factors at work: nature and personality; competence, expertise and experience; management style; and, not least, the past record of success. Even appearance plays a part. And, certainly, another important element is communications style and ability.

A manager who never has time for anyone, especially for consultation, and who conducts relationships through minimal, monosyllabic dialogue and terse, one-line memos, will rarely be viewed endearingly by others. Neither will a manager who waffles, who never expresses a real opinion, or who never voices a clear statement.

Poor communication may be no fault of the message itself, but can dilute the good impression or good influence that a manager would otherwise make on the team. It is difficult for people to accept even the most sensible message when it is buried (for instance) in a densely written report notable only for its length, its profusion of gobbledegook and 'officespeak', and its convoluted structure. Similarly, people are very harsh about certain methods of oral presentation: they are unlikely to say, 'What excellent ideas. What a pity they were not better presented.' They are more apt to say, 'What a rotten presentation. I bet the ideas were not up to much either.'

The converse is also true, of course. Good communicators are inherently more likely to be held in respect. What they say is, almost automatically, treated as reliable and credible. Confidence and competence in communicating are picked up by the recipients, who are more likely to pay attention, and to think about and give real consideration to messages they judge to be well conceived and directed. This will directly help the results of those who are seen in this positive light.

The foregoing is an effect that operates actively. In other words, people look at those communicating with them and actively seek to use their style and approach to assist in the judgements they make about content. If you doubt this happens, think of what occurs when even appearance contributes something very specific to meaning. If a voice says 'Excuse me' as you walk down the street, then your reaction surely takes immediate account of the fact if you turn to see it was said by an uniformed police officer.

The moral here is to act to ensure that you develop and use communications skills in a way that gains this kind of effect, even if it means sometimes operating with more confidence than you may feel!

Seeking after excellence

In many aspects of business today, just achieving an adequate performance is not enough. Competitive pressures have never been greater, and this has a ready parallel with organisations outside the commercial sector of the economy. A university, for example, has just as many pressures arising from the financial side of its operation as a company does in seeking profitability; indeed, some of its activities may have to operate on a straight commercial basis. Similar things apply to other kinds of organisation, from charities to government departments. As standards improve – in design, quality and service – then the broader market has to keep up and the effort needed to stay ahead increases. Excellence must be sought as standard to have any hope of competing in today's world.

All this extends the management job. Take a specific example. In customer service, when competition was less, a pleasant manner and reasonable efficiency shone out. Nowadays, those dealing with customers by telephone must offer product knowledge, technical advice and prompt service linked to very specific standards. They may well be required to answer the telephone within a certain time limit, operate complex computer equipment, see to the necessary documentation as they go, and send sales material to potential customers to arrive the following day, etc. – all in a manner that customers find spontaneous, courteous, informed and specific. This is no easy task. Nor is that of managing a section working in this way. Such a manager may need skills of administration, of computer systems, of marketing and of customer care, coupled with detailed knowledge of the products and customers. But whatever else is needed, skills in people management certainly are required – and also the communication skills that are an inherent part of them.

A *laisser faire* approach – one that primarily allows staff to work out their own methods and respond to the inherent customer pressure as they think fit – may not maximise effectiveness, although it might superficially seem an easier way of working for the manager in the short term. *Excellent* performance takes some more working at. Of course, the effects can be worthwhile – in this case, perhaps, in terms of customer satisfaction and thus future sales – but this effectively squeezes a larger management job into the same amount of time. This too is a problem, with managers in many companies these days frequently reporting that there is more and more to do in the time available, and generally with less people on their team than in the past.

There is no room for errors in communication to be allowed to reduce effectiveness in such circumstances, and there is every reason to use communication itself to enhance team effectiveness in any way it can. Good communication is a resource to be maximised.

➡ SUMMARY OF THE CHAPTER

Communication directly affects performance, and so there is every reason to make the best of it. In a busy life, many communications errors, inadequacies or omissions occur – not as a result of lack of knowledge or understanding but as a result of a lack of thought. Discussions are skimped; memos or reports are sent without being given the benefit of proper preparation; meetings are run *ad hoc* without clear objectives or agendas; and things are said on the spur of the moment that people live to regret later. Much of the problem is time. Other pressures seem to intervene, and rushing one item for the sake of another is seen as a – maybe unfortunate – necessity. Yet sorting out what occurs if things go wrong takes time too – sometimes more than can be saved by rushing.

Of course, communicating well also takes time. But there is no need for it to take much more than it would to communicate less well. What is more, any small amount of extra time so spent can be easily justified in terms of the impact on staff and the ultimate results that they achieve on the manager's behalf. Communicating effectively with staff means understanding and thinking of both what makes communication work and how staff view and respond to the whole process. It is to the latter that we turn in the next chapter, before going on to review the nature of staff communication in all its forms.

Chapter 2
What staff expect from their managers

I suppose leadership at one time meant muscles, but today it means getting along with people.

(Indira Gandhi)

Once upon a time, managers ruled supreme, employees hung on their every word and did as they were told – even if this was leaving their job as a result of *not* doing what they were told. If this was ever so, then it was a while back and there is certainly no merit in thinking such days will return. To recruit, retain and get the most from staff in today's economic and organisational climate means there is a need to treat them correctly.

Employees expect to be treated fairly, to be treated as if they matter, and to be consulted, involved and informed to a much greater degree than in the past. Some managers may resent the greater amount of time that all this takes. As has already been said, managing others *is* time-consuming. Although staff themselves might not list requirements in the same way as listed above, they nevertheless need more attention in a variety of ways – for instance, motivation, personal development, and sometimes a shoulder to cry on.

Communication is clearly part of all this. People relate their well-being in their employment to all sorts of things, of course, from the satisfaction they obtain from their actual work to the social interactions involved and what perks they are granted. Work is inherently bound up in people's feelings of self-worth and self-image – and, indeed, with the image others have of them.

➡ HOW VIEWS ARE FORMED

All employees (including managers) want to feel that their job enhances these feelings of self-worth and self-image. There are perhaps two particular aspects that concern people: the organisation that they work for and the manager to whom they directly report (and, in turn, the whole management culture and style of the organisation). The implications of each of these are discussed below.

The organisation

People are all different. Some want to work for a large organisation with the facilities, resources and opportunities that that entails; others find a smaller firm suits them better. Most want to think well of their employer and, if the organisation is well known, growing and/or innovative, employees may well draw strength from this. And this sense of pride is, incidentally, important to employees with regard to others as well as themselves. People like to be able to answer positively when friends and family ask about the organisation for which they work.

How do people arrive at a view about an organisation? This may seem a stupid question, but although some of it comes informally (the ubiquitous 'grapevine') and much comes through the interactions inherent in the work that individuals do, much is not apparent to employees unless they are told. Of course they will also see, if they look, communication aimed at others – advertising and other promotional material, for instance – but this and other such general communication may give only part of the picture and is not perceived as aimed at staff.

People look for clear, regular and pertinent communication directed specifically at them, and a policy to provide just that. Its being in place adds something useful and positive to working for any organisation, and it is usually very much appreciated.

The manager

If you are a competent manager, busily getting on with your job, you probably have little time to dwell on exactly what kind of manager you are. Indeed, if things are going well, there may seem little need for such introspection. However, *being managed* is wholly different. People think about their own manager (and others they may have directly to relate to or work with), and certainly rate being managed by a 'bad' supervisor as something that can sour even a good job and that is therefore to be avoided. Thus, whatever your (lack of) views about your own management style, you probably *do* have views – for good or ill – about your own manager. And so, of course, do those who work for you.

➡ THE 'IDEAL' MANAGER

The concept of the 'ideal' manager has been researched from time to time. Certainly there is a consensus on the factors that such surveys list, although some variance in what those who were asked ranked as first, second and so on.

One key factor that unsurprisingly comes at or near the top in most people's view is 'working for someone I learn from'. Management should always help build strengths and develop potential, and no one wants to experience working in a repetitive way that adds nothing as time goes by. As the old saying has it, it is better to have five years' experience than one year's experience repeated five times.

Other characteristics that people like in their managers include their being:

- fair
- consistent
- honest
- willing to give time to their people
- a good listener
- good at their job
- decisive
- consultative
- able to delegate
- prompt in dealing with matters
- able to see the broad picture and others' points of view

- challenging
- trusting
- respectful, and – no surprise –
- a good communicator.

This last is seen as important in its own right, and is also a necessary characteristic if a manager is to be able to qualify in some of the other 'good manager' areas listed above.

➡ MOTIVATION MATTERS

So people like having 'good managers' and receiving 'good communication'. But so what? They are surely there to work rather than to enjoy themselves. To some extent this is true, but peoples' motivation *does* matter. That is because it is well-proven that well-motivated staff really do tend to perform better than their less-contented peers. Well-motivated staff achieve higher productivity and quality of work, tend to be more self-sufficient and certainly necessitate less management time being spent on sorting them out, keeping their noses to the grindstone or correcting their mistakes. Time spent on motivation is very worthwhile and the subject is worth a short digression before we move on.

The fact that the level of people's motivation influences how they perform may well seem common sense enough, and it may well also be borne out by your own experience. If people feel good about their job – what they do and the circumstances in which they do it – they are likely to do it with more enthusiasm. More effort is put in and more achievement results.

But what exactly is 'feeling good about the job'? The analogy of a glasshouse with a motivational 'climate' is a good one. There are many ways in which the temperature inside a glasshouse can be varied to give the plants the precise conditions they need in order to thrive. The windows or door can be open or closed; or painted white to reflect the sun; the heating system can be adjusted up or down; and so on. So too it is with people. There are many and varied influences that together result in employees having a particular level of feeling about their work (a feeling that may vary over time, of course and sometimes by the moment). Some factors exert a negative influence, some a positive one. All of this is investigated in more detail in Chapter 9, including briefly summarising the way Frederick Hertzberg defined this process in terms of what he called 'hygiene factors' and the overall principles from which springs an understanding of how to motivate people. Of course, there is more to motivation than this, but the main point in the context of the present review is that there is no simple fix; many factors are always involved.

For the manager, the active motivation of the team is – or should be – an ongoing part of their thinking and way of working. There is no magic formula. Throwing money at people (even if this was possible) is not the answer; indeed, payment gets listed in Chapter 9 as a negative influence because few people are ever satisfied with current pay. It is necessary to seek, find and practise a mix of motivational methods in order to create and maintain a healthy motivational climate.

Some actions, such as an incentive scheme, are designed and implemented solely to motivate. Much that acts positively, however, occurs through things making up the normal pattern of work – which you can execute with an eye on motivational impact – and many are minor in terms of time and cost. The classic example of the latter, appealing to people's need to achieve and have that achievement recognised, is just saying 'Well done'. That may be the simplest and easiest form of motivation possible, and yet how many of us can put their hand on their heart and say that we do it sufficiently often? (Honestly?)

Many motivational influences, including praising people's performance, act only by virtue of communication taking place. For example:

- *meetings* may be interesting, constructive and even fun, and thus they can act motivationally or be regarded as a waste of time and a sign of management's uncaring attitude
- *appraisals*, the conduct of which some managers find a chore, can be highly motivational if constructively handled, where people then look forward to their appraisal and expect to draw benefit from the process
- *secrecy* (or, more specifically, unwarranted secrecy) knocks one aspect of people's feeling of security and is thus demotivational

- *feedback and reporting* may well be a necessary form of communication, but if it is made onerous or not explained properly, then although the information may be successfully collected an element of demotivation may well result.

A manager who, in the eyes of their staff, fails to communicate – not being available, saying 'I'll get back to you' but never doing so, constantly delaying, or not explaining matters or instructions adequately – runs the serious risk of diminishing any level of positive motivational feeling that may be built up through other means.

Motivation and communication go hand in hand. Positive motivation is fragile and seemingly small shortfalls in communication can have dramatic effects on what and how people think. On the other hand, small influences and small additions to more significant communications can have a quick, easily achieved and positive effect. This may just be the feeling we all know comes with someone saying, 'Well done' or 'Good work'; or it may be something of more substance – for example, the company that changes the format of its annual report so that it makes more sense to employees and circulates it to them with a special letter designed exclusively for them. Both types of management action can expect to gain a motivational response that would otherwise not occur.

People really do expect to be motivated. They may not, if asked, put it in quite those terms, but they know and like the effects when they occur and when it is well-judged and hits the right spot. The theme of improved motivation will therefore run on through the remainder of this text (and is referred to again specifically in Chapter 9). When communications are well handled, the likelihood is that one of the, perhaps peripheral, effects will be that people will think better of the manager, the organisation or both.

➡ WORKING TO CREATE A POSITIVE VIEW

The bad-news syndrome

Newspaper writers have been heard to say that they are more inclined to print bad news than good, because that is apparently what people want to read. Something similar seems to happen with regard to image. No company, nor any manager for that matter, is all good or all bad. Realistically, the information and feelings people have of either are made up of a mixture of the two. Yet factors regarded as bad and negative can all too easily overpower the good, and even when the preponderance of the facts are good, bad points seem to jump out. Mud sticks – witness the way some corporate disasters linger in the memory, colouring views of an organisation long after the event.

So, in some companies the word is that management communication is bad. That is not what is stated overtly, of course; instead, people mutter thoughts such as: 'Nobody ever tells us anything', 'You can't trust a word they say', 'Information is always too little and too late – they seem to think we like being kept in the dark', 'I don't understand a word they say; they go on and on', 'But what's the point?', 'Have you heard the latest rumour?' Everyone has heard such mutterings, and many will admit to having joined in; sometimes the muttering becomes a shout. Yet the point is that this does not mean that all is bad. Some communications may be well handled, but the point is that they can be overpowered by what are experienced as bad examples, and may even be diluted by assumed bad practice that is no more than hearsay.

The point here is not to harp on the negative. There is clearly an opportunity in this situation. Consistent good communications creates a powerful culture – one that people like and respond to, one that brings the direct benefits of accurate communication and of acting as part of what produces positive motivation and thus commitment. This provides yet another reason to foster good communications. The same principal applies equally to individual managers as well as organisations – something that should give everyone pause for thought.

Compatibility of intent

Despite the potential problems in communication, the end result of thinking about these things and doing so with a clear eye on how things seem from the staff perspective is positive. By trying to match your communications style with that seen as most acceptable by others, you gain positively in a number of ways. Thinking of even a small number of simple examples shows how this is so. You should make sure your communications have the following features:

- *Timeliness*. Rather than being seen to delay (with news of some new development, for example), people appreciate it when you avoid the rumours that inevitably accompany things seemingly kept back for no good reason.

- *Statements in the terms and language of those you are communicating with* yield a greater likelihood of understanding, and your efforts may add to a belief that there is no 'them and us' syndrome.

- *Openness*. It is good to take people into your confidence, rather than being dismissive or secretive towards them. You get attention rather than only prompting people to wonder whether or not there is not more to an announcement than meets the eye. It also means that, when you must be secretive (and there will be some circumstances when this is necessary), it is more likely to be regarded as justified; even more so if you quote a valid reason. Then people will be more inclined to be patient rather than kick-starting the rumour machine and putting it into overdrive.

With more major communication occasions, the same matching of communications style can often readily occur. For example, in matters of discipline, an immediate, short, sharp reprimand will often both nip a problem in the bud and be seen as fairer; whereas a period of fudge or hinting (perhaps while hoping the problem will go away) is resented, somehow seeming unfair even when there are understood grounds for some action to be taken. Similarly, meetings can be prime candidates for seeing things from others' point of view. Everyone knows from their own experience just how dire meetings can on occasions be – tedious and unconstructive, sparking confusion or conflict when they should be achieving something positive. Every manager who has felt this about meetings that have had to be endured should ask what people think of such meetings. Really. Even the ones where time was a problem, where there were other priorities preventing proper preparation, where contention over a minor issue nudged a major issue into second place, where the decision made proved ill-thought-out, where . . . But you get the point I am sure.

➡ SUMMARY OF THE CHAPTER

The moral here needs to be borne in mind throughout the process of managing: management is not something you do in a vacuum but is an interaction with other people. Both parties' feelings and attitudes are important, and it is for the manager to take the initiative in creating a way of working that allows for this fact and, equally important, is seen to do so. This perspective is certainly kept in mind throughout the text that follows.

Next we look at some of the difficulties that are inherent in the very process of communication. The factors here provide an overriding example of the need to keep everybody's situation in mind.

Chapter 3
Communication – pitfalls and opportunities

I do not mind lying, but I hate innacuracy.

(Samuel Butler)

Once in a while it is worth going back to basics. Think for a moment: how would you explain to someone (without demonstrating) how to tie a necktie? How many times have you heard someone in your office say something like 'But I thought you said . . .'? What is the difference between saying something is 'quite nice' and saying that it is 'rather nice'? And would you find anything that warranted either description the least bit interesting? Make no mistake; communication can be difficult.

Have you ever come out of a meeting or put the telephone down on someone and said to yourself, 'What's the matter with that idiot? She doesn't seem to understand anything'? And, if so, did it cross your mind afterwards that maybe the difficulty was that *you* were not explaining matters as well as you could? No? Should it have done? Make no mistake; the responsibility for making communication work lies primarily with the communicator. So, no surprise that the responsibility for getting through to your staff, for ensuring that things are clear is – yours.

The first rule about communication is never to assume it is simple. Most of the time we spend in our offices is taken up with communicating in one way or another. It is easy to take it for granted. Occasionally we are not as precise as we should be; but, never mind, we muddle through and no great harm is done. However, occasionally harm *is* done; some communication breakdowns become out-and-out derailments. For staff communications, where there is so much hanging on them, these must be got right and the penalties of not so doing range from minor disgruntlement to, at worst, major disruption to productivity or quality of work.

So the second rule is that everyone needs to take responsibility for their communication and to tackle it in a sufficiently considered manner in order to make it work effectively. This approach must make particular sense for all those managing people.

To set the scene for everything that follows, we will now consider certain key influences on whether communication works effectively or not. This chapter is unashamedly based on a similar review in my book *Communicating with Customers* (also in the *Toolkit* series published by Orion Business Books). So if you have read that book, you may find some duplication (though a reminder might perhaps be useful); and if you have not, then go out and buy a copy at once!

➡ THE DIFFICULTIES

If there are difficulties – and there surely are – then it is not because other people, or staff in particular, are especially perverse. Communication is, in fact, *inherently difficult*. Let us consider why.

Inherent problems

In communicating with staff, what you do is essentially a part of the process of achieving job objectives. As such, your intentions are clear and it is necessary to make sure people:

- hear what you say, and thus listen
- understand, and do so accurately
- agree, certainly with most of it
- take action in response.

Such action could be a whole range of things, from agreeing to spend more time on something, to attending a meeting, to following specific instructions. Let us consider the areas above in turn and in particular highlight the difficulties that might arise for each communication objective.

Objective: to hear/listen (or read)

People cannot or will not concentrate for long periods of time, and so this fact must be accommodated within the way we communicate. Long monologues are out; written communication should have plenty of breaks, headings and fresh starts (like this book); and two-way conversation must be used to prevent people thinking they are pinned down and forced to listen to something interminable.

Furthermore, people pay less attention to those elements of a communication that appear to them unimportant. Thus, creating the right emphasis, to ensure that key points are not missed, is a key responsibility of the communicator.

In other words, you have to work at making sure you are heard – to earn a hearing.

Objective: to ensure accurate understanding

People make assumptions based on their past experience. So you must make sure that you relate to just that. If you wrongly assume certain experience exists, then your message will not make much sense. (Imagine trying to teach someone to drive when they have never sat in a car: 'Press your foot on the accelerator.' 'What's that?')

In addition, jargon is often not understood. So think very carefully about the amount you use and with whom. Jargon is 'professional slang' and creates a useful shorthand between people in the know – for example, in one organisation or one industry – but it dilutes a message if used inappropriately or used in a way that assumes a greater competence than actually exists. (And remember that people do not like to sound stupid and may well be reluctant to say, 'I don't understand', which is something that can apply whatever the reason for a lack of understanding.)

Furthermore, assumptions are often drawn before a speaker finishes. The listener is, in fact, saying to himself or herself: 'I'm sure I can see where this is going', and then the mind reduces its listening concentration, focusing instead on planning the next response. This too needs accommodating, and where a point is a key feature then feedback can be sought to ensure that concentration has not faltered and the message really has got through.

It should be noted that things heard but not seen are more easily misunderstood. Thus anything that can be shown visually may be useful; so too is a message that 'paints a picture' in words.

Objective: to stimulate feedback

Some (all?) people sometimes deliberately hide their reaction to what they hear. Thus, some flushing-out and reading between the lines may be necessary in order to discover whether or not your hearers are agreeing with what you are putting to them.

Appearances can be deceptive for other reasons. For example, phrases such as 'Trust me' are as often a warning sign as a comment to be welcomed, and some care is necessary when dealing with people who make such reassuring (but maybe double-edged) statements.

Objective: to prompt some action

It is difficult to change people's habits. Recognising this fact is the first step to achieving it. It also means that better care must be taken to link the past with the future. For example, instead of saying, 'That was wrong and this is better', it is preferable to say, 'That was fine then, but this will be better in future' (and explaining how changed circumstances make this so). Any phraseology that casts doubt on someone's earlier decisions should be avoided wherever possible.

There may, of course, be fear of taking action: 'Will it work?', 'What will people think?', 'What will my colleagues think?', 'What are the consequences of it not working out?' This risk avoidance is a natural feeling, and so recognising it and offering appropriate reassurance is vital.

Many people are simply reluctant to make prompt decisions. They may need real help from you, and it is a mistake to assume that laying out an irresistible case and just waiting for the commitment is all there is to it.

The net effect

The net effect of all this is rather like trying to get a clear view through a fog. Communication goes to and fro, but there is a filter between the parties such that not all of the message may get through. Some information may be blocked out, some may be warped or let through only with pieces missing. In part, the remedy to all this is simply watchfulness. If you appreciate the difficulties, you can adjust your communication style a little in order to compensate, and you will achieve a better level of understanding as a result.

One moral is surely clear. Communication is likely to be better for some planning. This may only be a few second's thought – the old premise of engaging the brain before the mouth (or writing arm) – through to making some notes before you draft a memo or report, or even sitting down with a colleague for a while to thrash through the best way to approach something.

We have already tried within the last few paragraphs to provide some antidotes to the inherent difficulties, but are there any principles that run parallel and provide mechanisms to balance the difficulties and make matters easier? Luckily the answer is 'yes'.

➡ AIDS TO GOOD COMMUNICATION

Good communication is, in part, a matter of attention to detail. Just using one word instead of another can make a slight – even a significant – difference. And there are plenty of other factors that contribute to good understanding, many of which are explored as this book continues.

But there are also certain overall factors that are of major influence and that can be used to condition your communications. These include:

- 'What's in it for me?'
- 'That's logical'
- 'I can relate to that'
- Again and again.

These influences are described in turn below.

'What's in it for me?'

Any message is more likely to be listened to and accepted if the way that it affects each individual is spelt out. Whatever the effect, in whatever way (and it may be several ways), people want to know 'What's in it for me?' and 'How will it hurt me?' People are interested in both the potentially positive and the potentially negative effects of any proposals.

For example, you may tell someone that you have a new computerised reporting system that is to be implemented shortly, and they may well think the worst. Certainly, their reaction is unlikely to be simply 'Good for you' and more like 'Sounds like that will be complicated' or 'I bet that will take up more time'. Tell them they are going to find it faster and easier to submit returns using the new system and add that it is already drawing good reactions in another department and you are then starting to spell out the message and what the effects on them will be together, rather than leaving them wary or asking questions.

Whatever you have to say, bear in mind that people will view it with their self-interest in mind. Build in the answers to their implicit questions and you avert potential suspicion and make your listeners more likely to want to take the message on board.

'That's logical'

The sequence and structure of communication is very important. If people can see clearly what is being proposed, understand why it is chosen for the organisation, and believe it will work *for them*, then they will pay more attention. Conversely, if it is unclear or illogical then they will worry about it, and this takes their mind off listening. For instance, it might be possible to have an extra chapter (12) at the end of this book that (at rather a late stage) investigates the fundamental principles of communication and the reason for it, but I doubt whether it would be well received because the reason for having such a chapter, and placing it at the end, would be unclear to readers.

Information is remembered and used in an order – you only have to try saying your own telephone number as quickly backwards as you do forwards to demonstrate this. So your selection of a sensible order for communication will make sense to people, and that will help them warm to the message. Using an appropriate sequence helps gain understanding and makes it easier for people to retain and use information.

Telling people about this is called signposting. Say, 'Let me give you some details about what the reorganisation is, when the changes will come into effect and how we will gain from it' to your staff and, provided that makes sense, they will *want* to hear what comes next. So tell them about the reorganisation and then move on. It is almost impossible to overuse signposting. It can lead into a message, helping to give an overview, and it can also separately lead into subsections of that message. Sometimes it can be strengthened by explaining why the order has been chosen: 'Let's go through it chronologically. Perhaps I could spell out . . .'.

Whatever you have to say, think about what you say first, second, third and so on, and make the order you choose an appropriate sequence for the staff to whom you are communicating.

'I can relate to that'

Imagine a description: 'It was a wonderful sunset.' What does it make you think of? Well, a sunset, you may say. But how do you do this? You recall sunsets you have seen in the past and what you imagine draws on that memory, conjuring up what is probably a composite based on many memories. Because it is reasonable to assume that you have seen a sunset and enjoyed the experience in the past, I can be fairly certain that a brief description will put what I want in your mind.

It is, in fact, almost impossible *not* to allow related things to come into your mind as you take in a message. (Try it now: and *do not* think about a long, cool refreshing drink. See.) This fact about the way the human mind works must be allowed for and used to promote clear understanding. On the other hand, if I was to ask you to call to mind, say, the house in which I live and describe it to you not at all, then it is impossible for you to conjure up an accurate picture – at least unless you have been there or discussed the matter with me previously. All you can do is guess, wildly perhaps: 'All authors live in a garret' or 'All authors are rich and live in mansions' – and you would be wrong on both counts!

So, with this factor also inherent to communication, it is useful to try to judge carefully people's prior experience; or indeed to ask about it if they have not worked for you for long and you are unsure of their past experience. You may also refer to it with phrases linking what you are saying to the experience of the other person. For example, saying things like 'This is like . . .', 'You will remember . . .', 'Do you know that . . . ?' or 'This is similar, but . . .' are all designed to help the listener grasp what you are saying more easily and more accurately.

Beware of getting at cross-purposes because you think someone has a frame of reference for something that they do not. Link to their experience and use it to reinforce your own message.

Again and again

Repetition is a fundamental help to grasping a point. Repetition is a fundamental help to . . . Sorry! It is true, but it does not imply just saying the same thing, in the same words, repeatedly. Repetition takes a number of forms:

- things repeated in different ways (or at different stages of the same conversation)
- points made in more than one manner: for example, being spoken and being written down
- summaries or checklists used so as to recap key points
- reminders over a period of time (maybe varying the method – phone, fax, meeting, etc).

This can be overdone (as in the introduction to this point here), but it is also a genuinely valuable aid to getting a message across, especially when used with the other factors now mentioned. People really are more likely to retain what they take in when they hear it more than once. But enough repetition.

➡ POSITIONING YOUR COMMUNICATION

So far in this chapter the principles outlined have been general; they can be useful in any communication, not solely those with staff. But staff are a special category. If you want people to work willingly, happily and efficiently for you, one useful approach to any staff communication is to remember not to allow your communication style to become too introspective. If you want to influence them, relate to them in a way that makes *them* the important ones. Although you speak for the organisation, staff do not appreciate an unrelieved catalogue that focuses predominantly on your side of things. So try to avoid overuse of phrases such as 'the organisation is . . .', 'we have to make sure that . . .', 'I will be able to . . .', 'our service in the technical field is . . .' or 'my colleagues in research . . .' and use instead phrases that are turned round to focus on the employees. Thus: 'You will find this change gives you . . .', 'You will receive . . .' and 'You can expect that . . .'.

A slight mixture of phrasing is, of course, necessary, but a predominantly introspective approach always seems somewhat relentless. And it is more difficult when phrasing things that way round for you to give a real sense of tailoring to what you say to the individual because introspective statements sound very general. Using the words 'you' or 'yours' (or similar) at the start of a message usually works well, and once this start has been made it is difficult for you to make what you say sound introspective.

Projecting the right impression

Having made a point about not sounding too introspective, on the other hand you do need to be concerned about the image you put across; because there is a good deal more to it than simply sounding or appearing pleasant.

By all means compile your own list of important features for giving the right impression, but you will probably want to include a need to appear:

- efficient
- approachable
- knowledgeable (in whatever ways the customer expects)
- well-organised
- reliable
- consistent
- interested in your staff
- confident
- expert (and able to offer sound advice).

Staff like to feel they are working for someone competent – someone they can respect (see comments about the 'ideal' manager in Chapter 2). Fair enough. But the thing to note is that there is a fair-sized list of characteristics that are worth getting over, and all of them are elements that can be *actively* added to the mix. You can *intend* to project an image of, say, confidence and make it more than you feel, or of fairness when you want it to be absolutely clear that this is what you are being. Projecting the right mix – and balance –

of characteristics to create the right image is important. There is
some complexity involved here and thus it is another aspect of the
whole process that deserves some active consideration.

In addition, you must have a clear vision of the kind of way you
want to project the organisation you represent, as well as the
particular department or function you are in. This is especially
important when you are dealing with people with whom you have
less than day-to-day contact, such as those in other departments.
Consider whether an appearance of:

- innovation
- long experience and substance
- technical competence
- having a very human face
- confidence.

should be put over. Or whatever else. Again, you must decide the list
that suits you, and draw on it as appropriate so as to create the total
picture that is right for your set of circumstances. This is often no
more than just a slight exaggeration of a characteristic, but it can
still be important.

In all these cases, different levels and types of staff will need
different points emphasised in different ways. Some may warm to
an experienced manager with apparent concern for his or her staff,
and if so then any qualities creating that impression can be stressed.
Others may seek a more weighty commitment; so a style with more
telling involved makes sense for them and you will need to project
the clout to make it stick.

Individually, all the factors mentioned in this chapter are
straightforward. Any complexity in making communication work
comes from the need to concentrate on many things at once. Here
habit can quickly come to our assistance. There is a danger in this
too, however. Unless you maintain a conscious overview it is easy to
slip into bad habits or, by being unthinking – making no decision
rather than making the wrong decision – to allow the fine tuning
that makes for good communication to go by default. Remember
just a word or two can make a difference. A complete message
delivered in an inadequate manner may cause chaos.

One other key factor has not yet been given sufficient weight. As we communicate, we have to work at what occurs in both directions. There must be listening.

➡ LISTENING

Clearly, listening is vital – but it is not enough just to say that. You need to make listening another *active* process. This involves:

- listening very carefully
- concentrating on listening
- taking note of what is said (mentally and/or writing notes) and appearing to be a good listener and, above all,
- adapting how you proceed in the light of the information other people give and – an important element of this – being perceived to do so.

Few things endear a manager to staff quite so much as their marking you down as a good listener. It is a factor that needs only a little thought and can quickly become a habit (more of this later). Meanwhile, we turn to other factors that set the scene and are valuable in communicating with staff.

➡ THE 'GRAPEVINE'

There is one aspect of communication that creates both pitfalls and opportunities and that should be touched on and added for consideration at an early stage. This is the so-called 'grapevine': the network of informal information channels that exists in every organisation.

The grapevine takes many forms. In one office in which I worked, the main channel operated through the tea lady. As she moved throughout the offices during the day, news – good and bad, accurate and inaccurate – went with her. This was not so much her intention as reflecting the fact that people knew the channel existed and used it unashamedly. She provided an easy, reliable way to disseminate news; it became one that everybody found a major source.

There are some who regard the grapevine as an inherently 'bad thing', a catalyst to rumour and to be stamped out. Getting rid of it in an organisation is akin to nailing jam to the wall, however; it just cannot be done. So, how should you react to the grapevine? Simple: you identify how it operates and get plugged in. The alternative is missing a good deal of information (or catching up with it later than others) and removing from your use one potential way of communicating. It is not enough just to listen: given the nature of what is happening, you must learn to 'read between the lines'. Not everything you will hear will be true, some may be exaggerated and some may contain just a hint of something important. The main pitfall is in overreacting to things, without first checking and then finding you are dealing with hearsay, half-truth and rumour. The first rule is therefore to execute caution. But it can also prove, or be made to prove, a real asset.

The grapevine may be ubiquitous, but you need to approach it actively to make the most of it. First, as has been said, check out how it operates. The informal channels mean that anything may be contributing (like the tea lady), you need the ear of those who knowingly contribute, and you need to recognise – and make allowance for – the gossips. You need to watch for motivations, because sometimes the grapevine may be used maliciously. Be careful; it is one thing to be well informed and another to get sucked – perhaps unwittingly – into intrigue that may get you marked down as a troublemaker or overtly political.

The two best uses for the grapevine are perhaps to float initial information, as with the kind of information that is characteristic of changing attitudes, and to reinforce other communications methods, adding repetition in grapevine form to more formally introduced messages. The grapevine can even be used to communicate with individuals. For example, you might have a member of staff who has a problem with timekeeping. A few general remarks about its importance or about the danger of people being 'passengers' may be relayed onto the grapevine, reach the individual's ears, and lead to a change in behaviour before you have to communicate more formally.

Whatever your need and purpose in communication, the grapevine may have a role to play. Use it wisely – and do use it.

➡ A QUESTION OF QUESTIONS

Before moving on, we will include in this chapter some comment on a technique that is common in providing assistance with many of the forms of communication we will go on to review in succeeding chapters: that of questioning.

Many communication situations need to be clarified by the asking of questions. Unless you know the facts, unless you know what people think and, most important of all, unless you know *why* things are as they are, taking the process on may be difficult or impossible. How do you resolve a dispute if you do not really understand why people are at loggerheads? How do you persuade people to action when you do not know how they view the area in which you want them to get involved? How do you motivate if you do not know what is important to people or what worries them? The answer in every such case might be stated as 'with difficulty'. Questions create involvement, they get people talking, and the answers they prompt provide the foundation for much of what makes communication successful.

But questioning is more than just blurting out the first thing that comes to mind. 'Why do you say that?': even a simple phrase may carry overtones and people wonder whether you are suggesting that they should not have made the statement or whether you see no relevance of the point made. In addition, many questions can easily be ambiguous. It is all too easy to ask something that, only because it is loosely phrased, prompts an unintended response. Ask 'How long will that take?' and the reply may simply be 'Not long'. Ask 'Will you finish that before I have to go to the meeting at eleven o'clock?' and, if your purpose was to be able to prepare for the meeting accordingly, then you are much more likely to be able to decide exactly what to do.

Beyond simple clarity, you need to consider and use three distinctly different kinds of question:

- *Closed questions*. These prompt rapid 'yes' or 'no' answers, and are useful both as a starting point (they can also be made easy to answer to help ease someone into an in-depth questioning process) and to gain rapid confirmation of something. Too many closed questions, on the other hand, create a virtual monologue in which the questioner seems to be doing most of the talking, and this can be annoying or unsatisfying to the other person.

- *Open questions*. These cannot be answered with a simple 'yes' or 'no' and typically begin with words such as 'what', 'where', 'why', 'how', 'who', 'when' and phrases such as 'Tell me about . . .'. Such questions get people talking, they involve them, and they generally like the feel they give to a conversation. By prompting a fuller answer and encouraging people to explain, they also produce far more information than closed questions.

- *Probing questions*. These are a series of linked questions designed to pursue a point. Thus, a second question that says 'What else is important about . . .' or a phrase such as 'Tell me more about . . .' gets people to fill out a picture and can thus produce both more detail and the reasoning behind more superficial answers.

It is important to give sufficient time to the process when finding out is necessary. It may also be important to give the clear impression to staff that sufficient time is being given to something. This may indicate, say, the importance with which something is regarded; and the reverse may give the wrong impression – say of lack of concern. Both aspects may be important, and this is something that it may sometimes be useful to spell out: 'I want to go through this thoroughly. I can take an hour or so now, and if that proves inadequate, we can come back to it on another occasion. Let's see how we get on.'

Listening (again)

Asking things is one thing. Listening is something else. Staff want a manager to be a good listener. Managers need to be good listeners – the dangers of proceeding on assumptions or inaccurate information should be clear. It is partly a matter of courtesy and partly a matter of credibility: you will never be felt to be taking something seriously if you appear unwilling to listen.

The need here is to really work at listening. The following list, reproduced from my book *Career Skills – A guide to long-term success* (Cassell) sets out the essentials.

- *Want to listen*. This is easy once you realise how useful it is to the communication process.
- *Look like a good listener*. Staff will appreciate it and if they see

they have your attention, feedback will be more forthcoming.

- *Understand*. It is not just the words but the meaning that lies behind them that you must note.

- *React*. Let people see that you have heard, understood and are interested. Nods, small gestures, signs and comments will encourage the other person's confidence and participation.

- *Stop talking*. Other than small acknowledgements, you cannot talk and listen at the same time, so do not interrupt.

- *Use empathy*. Put yourself in the other person's shoes and make sure you really appreciate their point of view.

- *Check*. If necessary, ask questions promptly to clarify matters as the conversation proceeds, for an understanding based even partly on guesses or assumptions is dangerous – but ask questions diplomatically and do not say 'You didn't explain that properly'.

- *Remain unemotional*. Too much thinking ahead – 'However can I overcome that point?' – can distract you.

- *Concentrate*. Allow nothing to distract you.

- *Look at the other person*. Nothing is read more rapidly as disinterest than an inadequate focus of attention.

- *Note particularly key points*. Edit what you hear so that you can better retain key points manageably.

- *Avoid personalities*. Do not let your view of a member of staff distract you from the message.

- *Do not lose yourself in subsequent arguments*. Some thinking ahead may be useful; too much and you suddenly may find you have missed something.

- *Avoid negatives*. To begin a discussion with clear signs of disagreement (even a dismissive look) can make the other person clam up and destroy the dialogue.

- *Make notes*. Do not trust your memory, and if it is polite to do so, ask permission before writing comments down.

Listening successfully is a practical necessity if you are to excel at your own communication with your people.

With the need for effective questioning and listening skills – and all the factors raised in this chapter – in mind, we can now turn to the various specific circumstances in which communication with staff is important. We start at the beginning, with recruitment and selection.

Chapter 4
Recruitment and selection

You can rent a brain, but you can't rent a heart. The candidate has to throw that in for free.

(Mark H. McCormack)

The language is full of sayings such as 'first impressions last' and 'getting off to a good start', which show the importance of the first steps taken in many different circumstances. In managing people, the first opportunity to communicate with them is when new staff are being recruited. It is an important one: it influences the likely success of the recruitment-and-selection process and sets the scene for ongoing communication between each new recruit and the manager – and, indeed, the organisation.

Let us be clear: recruitment and selection is a vital task. You only have to think of the consequences of getting recruitment wrong to demonstrate this point. An inappropriate appointment – one that has to be changed – necessitates a large amount of work and cost (both monetary and emotional). What is more, some of the individual tasks involved are not the easiest to handle, as for example severing the appointment of someone who is failing to make the grade. It is difficult enough if the person is still in some prescribed probationary period, but it is worse if matters have been left longer. Then there is the need to advertise again, vet numerous application forms, conduct seemingly endless interviews and . . . but you doubtless get the picture. The greatest negative impact of all this may not be the inconvenience and cost, but the effect on the job being done – or not done – while all this goes on. Appointing the right staff needs care and a systematic approach.

Furthermore, the way things go can be directly influenced by the quality of the communication involved. One example is sufficient to show the truth of this. A badly worded recruitment advertisement may well fail to prompt replies from a suitable batch of applicants. It is clearly a waste if much of the vetting process is rejecting candidates who would never have applied in the first place if they had read a clearer statement of the brief. In the next section we review the steps involved in the recruitment process, commenting primarily on the communications factors that are inherent in them.

➡ A SYSTEMATIC APPROACH

There are eight stages to the typical recruitment process. These are as follows:

1. analysing the job and drafting a job description
2. setting matching criteria for the type of person who is most likely to be suitable
3. attracting candidates
4. assessing written personal details (application forms, CVs, etc.)
5. testing claims (e.g. checking references, administrating psychometric tests)
6. interviewing
7. additional meetings
8. making the final selection and appointing.

Each is now commented on in turn.

Analysing the job

The first step is being clear what the job is. It is easy to oversimplify this, saying only that a field salesperson 'must sell' or that a secretary should be able to 'handle the admin.'. The details need spelling out. What is the precise role? What tasks are involved? What is the overall job objective? A *job description* should be in writing and should spell out the details clearly. This is both a guide to recruitment and a guide to the successful applicant.

A job description should include and describe such details as:

- the job title
- reporting lines and working relationships
- primary and secondary objectives
- specific tasks (regular and occasional)
- standards and metrics relating to the job
- appraisal procedure
- remuneration and allied details.

(Note that I consider it beyond the remit of this book to spell out details of employment legislation in this context. Suffice it to say that clarity in such documents can be vital if employment matters should ever involve legal action.)

A good clear job description is the foundation of successful recruitment; and much more besides. Any thinking-through that is needed to produce this is time well spent. The job description focuses, unsurprisingly, on the job to be done. It provides the basis for the second document that is useful at this stage, that of a *personal profile*.

Constructing a personal profile

A *personal profile* sets out the characteristics of the kind of person who might be best qualified and able to undertake the job in question. The details that are useful here fall into four distinct categories:

1. *Basic personal characteristics.* Here, you can indicate criteria such as age, education, experience, special qualifications (e.g. fluency in a foreign language), availability, measurable skills (e.g. computer literacy or numeracy); all the factors, in fact, that are factual in nature. This section needs care: ask yourself why does the applicant have to have a university degree, be male, be aged 30–40 and be able to speak French? (Remember, too, that the use of some such characteristics links to employment legislation.) Apart from specifying what the job entails, the task is to restrict unlimited applications and make the selection process manageable. A balance is important here, because although you may want to trawl a wide area, you may not want to process the

applications of hundreds of people.

2. *Aspects of character*. These are important too, but clearly much more difficult to measure accurately. However, it is still worth being clear what would be useful – someone industrious, loyal, or gifted with great perseverance perhaps.

3. *Motivational factors*. Here, you look at what is likely to appeal to a person about the job. Will it suit someone who is ambitious, competitive, or what? Again, such factors act as a guide and are worth setting down clearly.

4. *Responsibility*. These factors are specific aspects of character linked to what might be called emotional maturity. Does the job need someone able to work on their own, care for others or with a streak of exhibitionism (that might relate to, say, a job demanding regular large-scale presentational tasks)?

Attracting candidates

There is a variety of sources of potential candidates in any recruitment. The sources include advertising, recruitment agencies, employment registers and many more; and this is not the place to review their relative merits. Suffice to say that whatever methodology is used, the job description that the jobseeker sees must be clear and attractive. If you write a job advertisement, therefore, you must make sure the copy is just that – and if you work through others (an agency, a personnel department), be sure they do not dilute or alter, albeit unwittingly, the descriptions you assign to aspects of the job.

The description will be improved if the wording of any job advertisement:

- avoids cliché superlatives (if you ask only for someone who is dynamic, enthusiastic, hard-working and creative, most people reading may say, 'That's me!', and the quantity of responses may be large, but the match with the job requirements may be low)

- describes the actual job to be done in a way that gives some feeling for how it would be to do it

- describes the organisation, both in terms of what it is and does and in terms of its style and culture – and does so openly: box numbers in particular reduce response drastically, and people may even worry that they are applying to their own employer

- quotes a specific salary or salary range (omitting this can halve the response)
- is clear about the nature and qualifications of the candidates sought.

Any deviation from these principles in what is probably a comparatively brief description risks a mismatch. Good communication at this stage ensures that applicants are mostly on spec. The next job is to sort out the best applicants and decide who goes forward to the next stage.

Assessing written details from applicants

Of course, applicants may not always be asked to write in. Initial screening can be done by telephone, and this can work well (given a tightly structured series of initial questions to identify the most suitable people amongst those who telephone). But, more often, the response is written and many organisations favour the use of an application form. This allows applications to be more easily compared one with another, because they are presented on a similar basis; a variation in CV format makes this more difficult, although such CVs can make good support material. Furthermore, many CVs have these days been prepared professionally and do not reflect so much of the candidate's character as when the individual has had to present information on the organisation's standard form (and covering letters are also worthy of study for the same reason).

Be careful of standard forms, however. The trick is to collect exactly the information *you* want, bearing in mind the position you are trying to fill. Thus it may well be worth producing one (that parallels the personal profile description) specifically, or at least amending a stock item supplied by the personnel department.

The guiding principle for application forms is that they should enable you to select those people sufficiently on spec to bring forward and become those offered an interview. The details completed on the form also provide a useful basis to cross-check information at the interview. Remember that people understandably put the best complexion on themselves in such documents (and at interview). Research shows that a significant number of people lie about their details (15% was reported by a newspaper carrying recruitment advertising).

The key point to remember is that the information you have to judge is not volunteered out of a vacuum by the candidates; you have prompted it. The way you describe the job, the way you design the application form, and the way you state what else you need (a covering letter, a CV, etc.) all contribute to how easy it is to prepare a short-list of candidates to call for interview.

Testing claims

There are potentially two stages involved in this aspect of the process.

First, *before the interview*, the key requirement is reference checking. If you use references (and surely you should) it seems a little pointless to spend time and money bringing someone to interview and then spending two minutes on the telephone discovering something that rules them out. This, like everything else, needs careful communication. The candidate needs to be asked for references (perhaps on the application form), and the reference needs to be asked for information that, first, checks facts ('Was she employed at your firm from October 1997 to September 1999?') and solicits opinion ('If circumstances allowed, would you re-employ her?'). A telephone call is usually more helpful than requesting a written response; people are busy and will give the matter little time, and are in any case often reluctant to commit certain comments to writing.

Second, *at the interview* there is an opportunity to test certain other kinds of information. For example, it should not be difficult to ascertain whether a candidate's French is as fluent as the individual claims, nor to explain and make acceptable the fact that this is being done. Other tests, of factors such as numeracy, may be a wise precaution and similarly need little explanation. Explanation is certainly important, however, if you use other kinds of test. A psychometric test may appear daunting, especially if a candidate is unfamiliar with such things. You are also asking, in some instances, for people to give up some time to such tests; this should be explained politely and thanks offered afterwards. Some elements, like the inclusion of psychometric tests, might usefully be mentioned ahead of the interview, for example in the letter agreeing time and place.

Whatever testing is done should augment your analysis and

judgement and not replace it, and this is especially so of the more 'fringe' areas of such things as graphology. Recruitment is seen by many people as something of a chore, but if there was a real shortcut – one 'magic' test that sorted the sheep from the goats – then we would all know about it! Sadly perhaps, making these kinds of judgement is not that easy.

Conducting the interviews

The interview is the most pivotal part of the whole process. Like any meeting, the interview needs planning and should have an agenda. Often, the application form is the best guide to how the interview should proceed. In view of the detail to be gone through, it may be useful to have a version of this (or its main headings) incorporated into a form that allows note taking. This provides the skeleton for the meeting.

A typical progression may then involve communication to cover:

- *a clear introduction*, designed to put the applicant at his or her ease and explain how matters will be dealt with, including a personal introduction of those present (together with their roles) on the interviewing side, a word about timing, and an indication of what action follows on from the interview)
- *clarification of the basic job details*, expanding on what may have appeared in an advertisement or been sent to the candidate
- *a first opportunity for the candidate to ask questions* about the job (although this stage should not be too protracted, and it is better to find out that someone is suitable before extending this stage)
- *an exploration of the candidate* and his or her capabilities (perhaps starting with their education, and covering work history, domestic, family and financial situation and anything else considered relevant). The detail here is important: for instance, not just who someone has worked for and what they did, but more specifically what they achieved and how – and indeed how they view it, what they learnt and how it equips them for the future
- once it is clear the candidate is a real possibility, it is appropriate to *add further details about the job and the organisation* – for

instance, how employment with the organisation works in relation to such matters as salary reviews and appraisals

- additional opportunities should be built in for *questions* as you proceed (while keeping close to the agenda and not allowing these to act as a digression – questions can always be held over to an appropriate moment)

- *a business-like conclusion* finalises matters, linking to the next actions and being as specific as possible – for example, some candidates might be told there and then that their application will not be pursued, whereas others might be given a specific date on which a decision will be made.

One further point is worth a mention here. Second opinions can, of course, be useful, depending on who gives them. Using multiple interviewers is a common technique, but can act not to secure the decision but to confuse. It should be made clear to the interviewee exactly who is present and what role each plays. If you are to explain this, it presupposes that you know! It is better to have a more formal arrangement than one based simply on saying, 'Sit in, would you, and see what you think'. Thus roles need defining, discussing and the way an interview is conducted must orchestrate the contributions of those present into a seamless conversation. It is particularly important that someone acts as chairperson (or it may appear that the left hand does not know what the right hand is doing) and that there is a designated note-taker. The worst scenario here is that after the interview *no one* is really clear what the next step should be, or can recall a particular – perhaps important – detail.

Additional meetings

Thorough initial selection, a well-designed application form, etc. and a suitable interview should reduce the necessity to bring back any but those on the shortest of short-lists for second or subsequent interviews. It may be that others who have a watching brief over recruitment need to be involved at some stage. It is worth making sure that this does not just become a formality (perhaps slowing and delaying decisions), or that it adds a wholly subjective element at a late stage. The senior person, wheeled in for a brief chat and saying simply 'I don't like them' may or may not have accurate judgement in such circumstances and thus may or may not help the proceedings.

However, any necessary secondary stages must be gone through with the same careful eye on the communications aspects that has applied earlier.

Making the final choice

This is the crunch point. Given the hazards of making the wrong decision referred to earlier, the first rule is perhaps similar to George Bernard Shaw's advice to those contemplating marriage: 'If in doubt, don't'. It really is sometimes better to start again and recruit more candidates than to appoint the best of a bad bunch who may prove inadequate. Decisions must be based on the information collected, perhaps categorising those short-listed into several batches (e.g. 'surpasses criteria', 'meets job criteria', 'meets most criteria', 'fails to meet . . .', etc.). Beware of 'feelings' taking over. Everyone likes to think that they are a good judge of character, but instant impressions are often wrong and, while less tangible measures are rightly a part of the decision, they should be kept in place alongside what is more measurable.

Finally, remember that people are likely to put on a good show at interview. Few prove wildly better than as they come over at the interview stage, and many will be a little less good than you may hope. You need to be firm in decisions here and not base too much on the hope that they will turn out better than you think.

➡ AFTER THE CHOICE IS MADE

The first job is something that is often ignored or glossed over, namely communicating with the unsuccessful candidates.

Communicating with the unsuccessful candidates

There is a final element of communication that is worth mentioning here and that goes beyond the eight steps already described. It is an old saying that 'courtesy costs nothing'. Yet courteous communication in this context does produce a worthwhile public-relations effect. So, always:

- reply to all the candidates
- say more than what will be seen as a 'token' few lines
- consider immediate alternatives (might they suit another opening in the organisation?)
- consider keeping them on file (and telling them you will do so).

Why this effort for people you are rejecting? Because they may be useful in future (maybe as customers rather than as job applicants); because they may talk, feeding positive or negative information about your organisation to others; and just because it *is* courteous and you are in a position to make them feel just a little better.

Communicating with the successful candidate

This should be as prompt as possible, and you should make all aspects of the offer clear. If certain details have to be left unresolved (e.g. a start date may be dependent on the candidate negotiating with the current employer about notice), then exactly how things will be dealt with and who will do what and when must be noted.

There should be a smooth link to the start-up stage of the new employee. Maybe another meeting is desirable before the individual starts; maybe they now need to read further information about the job or the organisation, or take other preparatory action. Whatever may be agreed should be confirmed. So, too, of course, should the administration of contracts, remuneration, etc. and some of this may deserve an informal explanation alongside the formal statements to make things clear – something that may be especially true of contracts.

There is no magic formula here. All the detail is important and little things can make a difference. For instance, many would recommend that the number of interviews held in a day is restricted to a level where indigestion of the wealth of information collected does not cloud judgement. Similarly, asking candidates to send photographs with their applications may help disproportionately the process of keeping in mind who is who as interviews progress.

Good communication throughout the recruitment process can link, for the successful candidate, to the communication involved in any induction process and briefing that takes place once the new employee takes up the appointment. This, too, needs to be well

planned and tailored systematically to cover whatever is necessary –
something that the specific job and person dictate. Induction
should not slavishly follow precedent.

➡ EXIT INTERVIEWS

Although it is, hopefully, a while after appointment that any
employee leaves the organisation, this is a convenient place in the
book to touch on the matter of what happens when people depart.
Remember, first, that some turnover of staff is both inevitable and
good. It is unlikely that any organisation can meet everyone's
ambitions for life, and if no one were to move on then it does not
say much for the quality of the team. A mediocre group may stay
longer, but is that an option you really want as a manager?

When people depart, it is useful to hold an exit interview with
them. People need to understand that this is not an attempt to
persuade them to stay (though you may want to try this!), nor is it
in any sense getting back at them for going. It is done solely with an
eye on the future. A chat at this stage, systematic in coverage yet
informally conducted, can provide information about what
employees:

- like and dislike about the organisation
- regard as changes that would potentially make it a better employer
- think of the culture and management style (and communications
  style – why not?)
- list as reasons for moving on
- see as the best strategy to replace them.

These and other similar areas of investigation can provide valuable
information.

One exit interview alone does not, of course, produce a definitive
picture. But the consolidated results of a number of such interviews
around the organisation (or even around a sufficiently large
department) can lead to action that improves staff retention, better
focuses recruitment and assists the process of staff motivation in
future. Such interviews are a useful form of communication. Their

conduct can easily be built into systems and procedures so that their occurrence is assured. Thereafter they represent time well spent.

➡ SUMMARY OF THE CHAPTER

A systematic approach to recruitment can save time and increase the likelihood of a successful appointment being made. It prevents the chore-like aspects of recruitment overpowering a truly well-considered decision-making process.

Attention to the clarity and detail of the communication process along the way acts as a useful courtesy to the unsuccessful candidates. More importantly, it acts as a precursor to the relationship that the newcomer will have with the organisation. It can usefully set the scene, giving each new employee an indicator of the communications style that will not only be appreciated by individuals but that they could do worse than emulate.

Chapter 5
Job appraisal

When a person tells you, 'I'll think it over and let you know' – you know.

(Olin Miller)

Between recruitment and the termination of employment there should come regular appraisals. These are usually annual, but sometimes a little more frequent. They will be formal or informal; and the first type may link to formal organisation-wide systems. All are a form of communication. All are an opportunity. This is so despite the fact that not everyone's experience of them is good. Nor is conducting them something that every manager looks forward to doing. Indeed, without the right approach they can be dissatisfying for all concerned. At worst they are seen as a time-consuming irrelevance that promises much and delivers nothing.

So, with the initial thought that appraisals should be constructive – helping employee and employer alike – we will take the formal systems first, and start by examining the reasons for the existence of appraisal systems. Why do they exist? One reason is that (in the UK at least) employment legislation says they must – or, rather, it makes it difficult to terminate someone's employment without showing how a person has failed to perform. If such a person has had no appraisal, the person may take the line of defence that no one has stated how performance in the job has been deficient.

Anyone wanting to avoid wasting time and money should avoid industrial tribunals like the plague; hence appraisal systems exist in most organisations. If this sounds pretty cynical, perhaps it is – it is no reflection on the need for positive employment legislation, but certainly it is a lost opportunity to see appraisals being conducted only for negative reasons. There are, of course, many positive ones. Such reasons include:

- reviewing each individual's past performance
- planning the future work and role
- setting specific individual goals for the future
- agreeing and creating individual ownership of such goals
- identifying development needs and setting up development activity
- on-the-spot coaching
- obtaining feedback
- reinforcing or extending the reporting relationship
- acting as a catalyst to delegation
- focusing on longer-term career progression
- acting to underpin or increase motivation.

Overall, the intention underlying all these kinds of thought is to ensure and improve future performance. The good appraisal takes the view that even the best performance can be improved, and seeks to increase the likelihood of future work going to plan and future results being achieved as planned.

➡ THE LINK WITH REMUNERATION

In the eyes of many people – and, indeed, in the way that many systems operate – there is an inextricable link between appraisal and salary review. In fact, most experts agree that a degree of distance is desirable. The objectives of appraisal are listed above. Of course the output of such discussions is useful in making assessments and decisions about salary. But the nature of the meeting can be compromised, and other discussions skimped, if the meeting is seen as a formality with the announcement at the end of 'So, we will be putting your salary up six per cent' being the only interesting part.

It is better, therefore, to separate the two things. An appraisal is just that, and salary announcements are made separately; albeit at a similar time of year. This prevents confusion, and maximises the effectiveness of both processes.

➡ PREPARATION

Like so much else, the key to effective appraisals is preparation. This should not just be in the sense of preparation just ahead of the meeting, and applies to both the appraiser and the appraisee.

The appraisee should be encouraged to prepare. The first step is to ensure that you communicate clearly and thoroughly the purpose and format of the appraisal. People should understand the need for it, its importance, the specific objectives it addresses and how both parties can get the best from it. It is a good idea to suggest that people prepare throughout the year. This may entail action as simple as keeping an appraisal 'collection' file. In this, people should note matters that can usefully be raised at appraisal and link those notes to the filing of copies of any documents that will assist the process. Without this action memory can be stretched to call to mind all the things that have occurred throughout a year and those that lend themselves to discussion at an appraisal. It can avoid opportunities for constructive discussion and review being missed.

The appraiser should likewise keep a file – one per person in this case – and should also plan in some detail the kind of meeting they intend to run. More of this in a moment.

First, we need a word about systems.

➡ FORMAL SYSTEMS AND MEASUREMENT

It is not the purpose here to specify exactly how the measurement aspect of appraisal systems should work; you may in any case not have the option of using other than what your organisation specifies – though you might want to influence things for the future. The measurement principles of any system nevertheless need to be made clear to those who will be appraised, and that is a communications task.

The basis used can vary, but it usually incorporates some form of rating scale. Topics chosen for measurement must be pertinent, and primarily that means linking them to the improvement of future performance. They must also be *perceived* to be relevant. As an extreme example of the wrong approach, I once saw a company appraisal form that measured 'honesty', giving it ratings just like other factors on a list from 1 to 10. Surely in most companies people are either honest or fired; and it is not a matter for appraisal time?

Five basic approaches are most common, and of course these are not mutually exclusive and can be used in various combinations. They are:

- *a simple numeric scale*: 1–6, 1–8 or whatever (an even number with no mid-point is favoured by many so as to avoid the temptation to mark everything as 'average'); such could equally be designated A–D or similar
- *a descriptive scale*: this may or may not be linked to numbers, and the words may or may not be chosen with precision, e.g. 'excellent', 'very good', 'good', 'fair', 'adequate', 'unsatisfactory'
- a graphic scale: this is effectively just a line with identified positive and negative ends, perhaps with scale marks (e.g. mid- or quarter-points) along its length
- *a comparative scale*: which might be a list of say 4–10 statements, e.g. phrases like 'better than most in the group'
- *a behavioural scale*: this rates a list of alternatives that specifically relates to things done, e.g. 'always', 'almost always', 'usually', 'infrequently' or 'never done'.

Ratings are important. They ensure consistency and fairness – something that it is useful to point out to appraisees.

Ensuring understanding

The communications job here is to create among staff a constructive attitude to the whole process. Such communications can start as soon as people join an organisation and must be in evidence when appraisals are due. The specific tasks include:

- explaining the rationale for appraisal
- setting out the specific objectives
- making clear the measurement aspects
- explaining the procedures and documentation
- briefing as to what action is required of the appraisee

- spelling out the advantages to both the organisation and the individual.

Only if both parties are clear regarding such a list are appraisals likely to be really useful. Once there is clarity in this respect, then the appraisal process can proceed. A systematic approach, and attention to detail, by the manager in both preparing and conducting appraisal meetings is still essential if the process is to be constructive.

➡ PLANNING AN APPRAISAL MEETING

The success of any appraisal has its roots in the thinking that proceeds it. As has been said earlier in this chapter, a manager almost certainly needs a way of collecting information and thoughts about each member of the team throughout the year. Appraisal is the end point of thinking that should span the year. Not only is it difficult for most people to recall every detail of someone's working year (more so for several somebodies), but being seen to be conducting an interview on the basis of incomplete information will cast the whole process in the wrong light, and at worst its credibility will be lost.

So, the manager must:

- spend sufficient time with people through the year
- keep clear records
- brief people on their role and what to expect
- assimilate (and explain) the documentation and systems
- prepare for each individual appraisal they will conduct.

What some of the time spent with people should consist of is investigated later in this chapter. Here, we continue to review the immediate preparation task. Background information needs looking into, and it may be that this includes: checking the appraisee's job description (which may need amendment after the appraisal); looking up specific objectives set for the past period; considering changes to the job, its responsibilities or other circumstances that need to be taken into account; and, of course, linking back to any previous appraisal meeting held.

Thereafter, a systematic approach will assist the process. You may well need to think about what suits you best, and what the system you use necessitates, but the following is intended to act as a guide to what might work best.

Before the appraisal interview

Steps might include:

1. *Prepare a written notification.* An explanatory note at this stage is the last chance to make sure people approach their appraisal in the right way. This means that as well as confirming a mutually convenient time and date, certain background information needs to be included as well (and perhaps copies of any documents or forms to be used or referred to during the meeting).
2. *Study the individual's file.* Indeed, go further if necessary, making sure that all information you need about what was supposed to be happening and what has happened is to hand. Make notes of points arising that need discussion and ensure that you can find your way around the file and documentation easily as the meeting progresses.
3. *Check performance factors.* This will include, for example, referring to agreed standards of performance and also to any such aspects that are no longer relevant, or in need of amendment or addition.
4. *Draft a provisional assessment.* This will comprise perhaps a page that will act as a starting point for the appraisal. Do not prejudge the discussion or make decisions on which it is dependent. These notes can act to prompt an agenda for the meeting – something that needs to link also to the way a system works.
5. *Critique your initial thoughts.* It is useful to ask yourself a firm 'Why?' about anything said at this stage. If there is no clear answer that comes to mind, then more research may be necessary or the fact may influence the line the appraisal meeting needs to take.
6. *Consider specific areas of the appraisal.* For instance, consider development. It may be clear at this stage that some training is necessary for the employee. Again, without prejudging the

issues, it may be useful to check out what might be suitable so that this can be incorporated into the discussion.

7. *Think ahead*. Remember that the most important part of the discussion will be about the next period. It may be useful to be planning particular projects and tasks for the future; especially perhaps those that foster development as well as simply reflecting operational considerations.

8. *Consult with others*. Where necessary to having a complete picture, it may be useful to consult with others about the person to be appraised, namely those who work or cross paths with that individual – from specialists like the training manager, say, to people in other sections.

9. *Check the rationale of your intentions*. In other words, make sure that you are able to answer the appraisee's question 'Why?' about anything that you plan to raise and discuss.

At this point you can move onto the task of making the appraisal interview go well.

➡ THE APPRAISAL INTERVIEW

In the interests of both efficiency and courtesy (which one can surely count as communication), you should set the meeting up to do it justice. So some of the first points here may seem obvious but are nevertheless important – and can easily be handled in a way that is less than ideal in a busy world. Bear in mind the following.

- *Allow enough time*, both to do the job and to give the right impression about the occasion. Few appraisals will be accomplished properly in less than an hour; some may last two or three hours (or more) and still be time usefully spent.

- *Allow no disturbances*. Nothing will more quickly give people the impression that you do not rate the event highly than allowing constant, or even occasional, pauses while you take telephone calls or deal with other passing matters.

- *Create a suitable environment*. Appraisals should be held somewhere comfortable – perhaps less formally than across a desk, yet with all the facilities required. Even something like the ability to balance and consult papers conveniently may be important if no desk is used.

- *Put the individual at ease.* Recognise that, even with good communication beforehand, appraisals may be viewed as somewhat traumatic (by both parties!). Everything that can be done to counter this (which includes some of the above) is useful.

The proceedings during the meeting also need care. Clearly this is an area of a considerable range of detail. Appraisals will vary given the circumstances, not least the role and function of the individual being appraised. The following therefore concentrate on the main general issues to be borne in mind.

To remember during the meeting

The following are pointers to be remembered during the appraisal interview itself.

- *Spell out the agenda and the way things will be handled.* This can usefully include asking what the priorities for the appraisee may be.
- *Act to direct the proceedings*, but do not ride roughshod over the other person.
- *Listen.* This is the most important activity. The appraisal meeting is primarily an opportunity for the appraisee to have his or her say. In a well conducted appraisal the appraisee should always do more of the talking than the appraiser, and the interview must be conducted on this assumption and to prompt it happening.
- *Keep primarily to performance factors.* It should not be your intention to indulge in amateur psychology or attempt to measure personality factors.
- *Use the system.* Most systems and most appraisal forms act as a guideline to the meeting; in other words, working through the form systematically will ensure most of what needs to happen happens.
- *Encourage discussion.* For example, personal strengths and weaknesses, successes and failures, and the implications for the

future can all be discussed. (See the paragraph about questioning techniques on page 35).

- *Set out action plans.* Those that can be decided at the moment should be spelled out (who will do what and when); those that need more deliberation should be noted in terms of when and how action will be taken. There may need to be a separate focus on each of a range of issues here, for example training and development action.

- *Tell people the basis of assessment,* and spell this out clearly (with reasons clearly identified if necessary). Be firm about decisions made.

- *Conclude on a positive note.* This should always include a 'thank you' for the part the appraisee has played in the process (and for the work undertaken in the last year!), and such a conclusion can usefully link to any subsequent documentation.

After the meeting

There is one key action here: to complete promptly any documentation and confirmation that are necessary after the meeting, and to send this to the appraisee, maybe flagging an opportunity for further discussion. Copies might have to go to departments such as personnel. You should also bring your own file up to date ready for next time.

Grasping the opportunity

There really is a major opportunity here. Good communication in the form of a sensible appraisal can act directly and positively to make more likely the chances of achieving good future results and hitting specific targets through each appraisee. Remember that the need to adapt and change is necessitated not simply by identifying and then strengthening weaknesses; there may be other reasons. In the modern world the need for individuals to change is as likely to be because of changes in a dynamic environment, where the changes that the appraisal is prompting are by no means a criticism of anything that has been done in the past, but rather are a planned response to changes that may have been impossible to predict or to prevent. On other occasions appraisal meetings must address changes that *are* predicted so as to ensure that people will be ready for them. This is a point that should be made clear to staff, who otherwise may feel that their appraisal reviews always have something of a witch-hunt about them despite the contrary indications.

Perhaps unfortunately in terms of the time the whole process takes, appraisal cannot be regarded as a one-off annual event. No manager can afford to heave a sigh of relief when appraisals are over and forget about them until the next year. So it is to the question of ongoing activity in this area – and its attendant communication – that we turn next.

➡ ACTION THROUGHOUT THE YEAR

It is possible to think of every contact – and every communication – throughout the year as potentially an ongoing part of the appraisal process. The main part of the activity, though, will be additional meetings to review progress. These may be 'appraisal-based', an overall review of performance, or 'project-based', where the appraisal opportunity comes out of the progressing of a specific project.

In either case the situation should be flagged to members of the team. It is clearly likely to cause problems later if a discussion that a staff member takes to be very informal (and a chance to say openly what that individual thinks) is then quoted in evidence later on in a formal context. If such an employee is only made aware at this later stage that the manager was noting things for appraisal purposes, this may well be resented – and perhaps rightly so. Many managers will, in any case, have an ongoing timetable agreed with their staff to continue the annual review in a variety of ways over the year. Some of the discussions that make up this process will be arranged, and timed, well ahead; others may take advantage of circumstances. In each case, both parties must be clear about what is happening.

The same principles as have been commended so far in this chapter apply to the ongoing process as well as its more formal annual manifestation. This means that matters such as giving due notice (and thus time to think or prepare), sufficient time for any meeting, and avoidance of any interruptions are again important. At least an appraisal meeting, even if interrupted, is a formal occasion. If an impromptu ten-minute session that might maintain the continuity of things is rendered useless by interruptions and has to be abandoned, then the whole opportunity may be wasted and the value of the process diluted.

The link to other activities

Finally, it should be noted that there is an overlap between the appraisal process as a form of communication and other areas of management communication. Four are worth specific mention:

- *Consultation and counselling*, which can occur for a multitude of reasons (and are dealt with in more detail in Chapter 8), can link positively to appraisal. For example, delegation can see someone working on a project that will unashamedly stretch that person's skills. Supervision is arranged, perhaps with some counselling alongside it. If a project involves someone in making a formal presentation for the first time, for instance, then help with preparation and a sounding board being provided at a rehearsal stage (as well perhaps as more formal training) may ensure that the final presentation is more likely to succeed. Training is involved, as well as support and guidance. The whole process is constructive and surely provides an insight into someone's performance that might – constructively – be linked back into the appraisal process.

- *Training and development.* This is tightly associated with appraisal; indeed, a prime reason for holding appraisals is to ascertain what training and development may be useful in future. Because training is often needed, not to correct faults but to extend skills or respond to new situations, the requirement for it may crop up at any time. Sometimes the need is unexpected and urgent. Thus this too is an ongoing process and overlaps with, and runs parallel with, the appraisal process. (The details on training and development are picked up in Chapter 7.)

- *Motivation.* The process of generating and maintaining an atmosphere of positive motivation amongst staff is important. Effectively done, it makes a real difference to attitude, commitment and results. Appraisal – the exercise of being appraised, that is – should be motivational. One of the prime reasons for ensuring that it is carried out well is to ensure that this effect is achieved. As appraisal is designed to improve future performance and high positive motivation creates the desire to want to succeed, the link is obvious. (Further comment is left until motivation is reviewed in Chapter 9.)

- *Feedback.* All of the foregoing is enhanced by feedback. The discussions that take place under these headings all assist each other. Thus, for instance: a positive training experience can lead to a next counselling session being more constructively approached, and more being achieved through it as a result. And this in turn can build motivation. Clearly, decisions about appraisal are affected by such chains of events. At the year end, one course of action seems clear, but subsequent events can change things such that the basis for the original decision is no longer valid. A planned action then has to be changed, and what happens next is tightly based on analysis of the current situation. Whatever else, appraisal must keep its feet firmly on the ground, as it were – it must reflect the real, up-to-date situation and it must never be allowed to be seen as a sterile, academic exercise.

➡ SUMMARY OF THE CHAPTER

For whatever reasons – and there may be many, such as unease with the process or inflexibility of the system – the opportunity of appraisals is often missed, or at least used less effectively than it might be. The opportunity here is considerable. The appraisal process is not only a vehicle for change, and one that can be a precise and powerful one; it is also a powerful agent in the culture of an organisation and people's attitude to it.

Getting this aspect of management communication right is not easy. But it is a challenge that deserves attention and one that, when met, potentially produces very worthwhile effects.

Chapter 6
Keeping in touch

Anything worth doing is worth doing to excess.

(Edwin Land)

There are probably more instances of communication with your staff throughout the year than you can even recall. It takes all forms, from formal meetings to a minute or two's quick word as you pass on the stairs. Indeed the informal can be an important part of the whole process of keeping in touch. Tom Peters and Robert Waterman, in their ground-breaking book *In Search of Excellence* (HarperCollins, 1995), coined the acronym MBWA, 'management by walking about'. It made the point that keeping in touch is something that has to be formally orchestrated through a variety of methods and then has to be worked systematically at to keep the whole process in play. The process of working at the informal in fact needs a formality.

While you can hardly have too much communication with staff (well, good communication anyway), all of it needs some care, particularly as apparently routine ongoing communication is often handled on 'automatic pilot', with little thought other than getting it done and moving on to greater priorities.

Here we review various aspects of this sort of activity, particularly through the medium of written communication and meetings. But we will start with some miscellaneous points about a mixture of different kinds of communication (all of which might be linked to the topics reviewed in Chapter 3).

➡ GETTING IT RIGHT

Remember that, as has been said, the responsibility for getting communication right – that is getting the output understood and acted upon – lies firmly with the communicator. Sometimes when we, for instance, emerge exasperated from a meeting saying, 'What's the matter – don't they understand even the simplest thing?', we might all ask ourselves why this is so. Perhaps the fault lies in the explanation rather than being a matter of poor reception.

Instructions

Much of what passes between a manager and staff is in the nature of an instruction. If so, the need is obvious.

Instructions must, first of all, be *clear*. Explanation may need some thought and it is very easy to find yourself going round the houses, making something up as you go along, and failing to get the core message over in an unambiguous way. Clarity is a fragile flower. One ill-judged word may be all that is necessary to create a problem: say 'Please do this immediately' and you may leave the urgency unclear; say 'Please drop everything and get this finished before lunch' and the request is much clearer.

Second, instructions must be *appropriate*. Each individual may need something a little different. If that individual's experience encompasses the subject, brief instructions only will be adequate; if instructions take the employee into a new area of expertise, then more detail or more background may be necessary.

Confirmations

Clarity and appropriateness are doubtless important here too. By confirmation is meant the need to put things in writing. The importance or formality of matters may indicate this need; so too may complexity. For example, such matters as the detail of someone's appointment or promotion, decisions following appraisals, and disciplinary matters should all be put in writing. So too should something like an agreed project timetable.

A few words may meet the need, or more may be necessary. Details of who has received such a note should appear on it. And, if you need to be able to show that something was sent, bear the method in mind (for example, e-mail can be – wittingly or unwittingly – erased at the touch of a button).

Reports and briefings

More extensive communication (documentation, meetings, written reports or presentations may all be indicated here) needs more thought. Perhaps the greatest guarantee of such communication working is for it to have clear objectives. This may be important for any communication, but is doubly so when greater length is involved.

Checking really is as easy as asking: 'Why am I doing this?' At this point in your mental responses to this, avoid vague statements such as 'The presentation is tell them about the office reorganisation' and keep asking questions. Why do they need to know? What detail do they need to know? What do you want to happen once they know? Do you want to prompt some action – and if so, what exactly and how is it to be done? How do you want those involved to feel – in agreement, pleased, enthusiastic, worried? And should the message change earlier feeling?

If you are clear as to why something is being done, and if you set clear objectives, then it is surely easier to plan exactly how to deliver the message. The alternative is the kind of rambling report that does no more than say 'something about' its topic and that is apt to be lacking in real structure, at worst moving from one 'and another thing . . .' phrase to the next with the recipient having little idea where it is all going.

In all such cases you need to think about the *communication methods* that might be used and pick the most appropriate to a particular circumstance. Ask yourself the following.

- Is significant feedback necessary (in which case perhaps it needs to be handled face to face)?
- Is some simple feedback necessary (such as a telephone conversation, perhaps)?
- Is it necessary to have a record (so that something in writing makes sense)?
- Is it a routine and informal communication (so that e-mail would suffice)?
- Does the complexity require a combination of methods (for example, a meeting, a telephone conversation to check details, and a memo to confirm)?

In every case, a plethora of different factors will affect the choice: urgency, complexity, formality, involvement of a number of people, and so on. Furthermore, every possible method needs to be considered. Choice should be made with regard to such criteria, and the temptation to do what is personally easiest must be resisted. It is very, very easy to, say, grab the telephone, have a brief word and then find later that confusion reigns and something more permanent was really necessary.

➡ PUTTING IT IN WRITING

The long-predicted 'paperless office' may seem as far off as ever to most of us, and there remains a need to 'get things down on paper' more often than most people would like. For many, writing is a chore. Somehow it takes more time and is viewed as more difficult than just telling people something.

Certainly, prevailing standards of business writing often leave something to be desired. Who has not struggled to read a report that lacks structure, but positively overflows with gobbledegook and 'officespeak'? You may long to be on the receiving end of material that is clear, succinct and easy to read; and so too do your staff, no doubt. Why is so much written material a struggle to read? There is one reason that is more important than any other.

This reason always seems to be made clear in courses that I run on various aspects of business writing. If participants are asked to write something, some at least will produce something poor. If some point is then picked up in analysis, and they are asked why it is written in a particular way, they do not justify it but readily accept that it could be better. What has happened is not that they have made a wrong judgement or thought about the thing in the wrong way, but that they have written it on automatic pilot and *thought about it little or not at all.*

Good business writing is what might be referred to as a career skill: something that not only enables you to get your job done effectively but that also helps build your image and your progression in your career. Certainly, staff are unlikely to warm to your communications skills if they feel you never use one word when ten can be used instead (or if they are unclear at the end of it about what you meant, however many words you used).

While you might conclude that this is an area worthy of more study (and I have written on it at greater length in *How to be Better at Writing Reports and Proposals* (Kogan Page, 1997), we shall concentrate here just on some key issues that make for better writing.

A focus on the reader

Your staff will want from you or your managerial colleagues something that is:

- *succinct*, i.e. as brief as content and purpose allow
- *understandable*: preferably easily understandable
- *precise*: saying what is necessary, unclouded by extraneous material
- *in their language*, and at an appropriate level of technicality
- *simple* in language and structure
- *descriptive*: letting language really add to the bare message.

Preparation

As with so much else, preparation is key. Before you turn away, rejecting thought of spending still longer before writing anything, let me say that I believe preparation is also a time saver. A little preparation should allow you to write better, but also to get it down faster. As has been said earlier, consider why you are writing and set yourself clear objectives.

Make a few notes of what you plan to say (and do not worry about sequence or anything else); then put some order to it, add a little more detail if necessary, and only then start to draft something. This preparation may only take a few seconds and be done on the back of an envelope, or it may be a longer process and more formal. (This book began life as notes on one large sheet of paper, divided into chapters, so that it was clear at a glance how one thing linked to another.) What you do when you work this way is important and useful: you separate the process of deciding *what* you will say, from that of deciding *how* exactly you will say it.

Most people find this is easier – when you start to draft something all you have to worry about is how you say it: you work to a content, structure and sequence that you have already considered and decided. If some editing is still necessary, do not worry – you are normal. Most people need to look back and make some alterations. So be it; the job is to make the communication effective. But work this kind of way and you will get progressively faster, and have to do less editing too.

Shape

The structure and sequence that you employ needs thinking about as you plan. Both should reflect the needs of the reader as much as the convenience of the writer. They should be logical (and the logic may need explaining); for example, often, in describing how a project will be run, a chronological sequence may make sense.

And both the structure and sequence should show in the end product. Use headings and also what I referred to earlier (in Chapter 3) as 'signposting', i.e. flagging that something is coming. For example, saying that we will move on from this paragraph of the book to comment on language and layout is signposting. So is saying that after dealing with putting things in writing we will turn to the matter of meetings; so, too, is the heading to come which picks up that point.

Language

This is no place for a treatise on grammar (though many would concur that this is important), but *language* is important. It should be:

- *clear*: the right words (are you writing about recommendations or options), the right phrases (what, exactly, is 'an immediate response'?) and the right arrangement and use (nothing can be about 12.74%, and if you begin 'At this stage . . .', then a later alternative is implied)
- *straightforward*: short words, short phrases and short paragraphs coupled with plenty of headings. Do not say the likes of 'at this moment in time' (for 'now'), or 'due to the fact that' (for 'because'). So, avoid sesquipedalians (an appropriately long word

meaning 'long words' – which my spell checker has never heard of)

- *natural*: writing that mirrors much of what you would say (and is formalised just a little) is better than an overstated 'written' style
- *relevant*: comprehensiveness is never an objective (not literally) and being succinct has already been mentioned
- *positive*: almost all communication with staff needs to be positive, there is rarely a place for 'perhaps', 'possibly' and 'maybe'
- *descriptive*: try to paint a picture and remember that the likes of 'as smooth as silk' will always be better than a wishy-washy 'it's sort of shiny'.

In addition, you should avoid writing that is:

- *too introspective*: not 'I', 'I', 'I' all the time
- *patronising*, and talks down unnecessarily
- *biased*, at least where it is intended to be otherwise
- *politically incorrect*: language has changed in this regard and continues to do so, so that asking someone to be chairman (rather than chairperson or chair) or similar may cause an upset and sound patronising even where that is not the intention
- *bland*: say what you mean – what exactly is a slight delay, or an attractive plan? Beware of phrases such as 'very nice'
- *old-fashioned*: we should no longer be using phrases such as 'enclosed for your perusal'
- *faddish*: words or phrases that are too new to be well known (and perhaps likely to enjoy only a short life anyway).

And avoid also obvious (and, for some, annoying) linguistic errors of which the following are just a few brief examples:

- *poor, punctuation* (sic)
- *tautology*: or unnecessary repetition as in 'I, myself, personally' or 'future planning'
- *oxymoron*: two-word paradoxes such as 'distinctly foggy' or 'a great little car'

and, my own pet hate, remember that nothing can be *very* unique: it is either unique or not.

Layout

Word-processing software allows the convenient use of all sorts of emphasis: **bold** type, *italics* and devices such as indenting, bullet points, boxed paragraphs, etc. as well as the classic UPPER CASE letters and simpler `type changes`. All should be used to add emphasis and allow space.

Just one practical factor will suffice to illustrate the need to consider layout. If something is to be discussed – a report perhaps – then it may well need to accommodate handwritten annotations conveniently and so a layout that allows plenty of space will work best.

No one should allow a lack of confidence or style to cramp their intentions with regard to written communication. The formats of the various mediums involved – reports, proposals, minutes, memos, e-mails, etc. – all contribute to the end result. All have their place. All too have their different nature, a fax seemingly more urgent than a letter (but being less impressive in appearance), an e-mail being quick and informal yet easily deleted and forgotten. It is a case of 'horses for courses' in a number of ways.

A little extra time and effort spent considering layout may well be worthwhile. How you write says something about you. It does no harm at all if people say things like 'Her reports are always good – you never have to wade through unnecessary minutes when she reports a meeting'. Being at least as good at written communication as at any other form is a real asset.

➡ MAKING MEETINGS WORK

This topic was signposted earlier. Meetings are ubiquitous. You are going to have to use them as a form of staff communication, so the only practical option is to make them work for you.

Meetings are not everyone's favourite organisational activity. Indeed, if I had a ten-pound note for every unconstructive meeting I have sat through over the years, I would have no need to be writing this! Meetings can be hard work, boring and end up serving no useful purpose. They can contribute nothing to advancing a topic or prompting a decision.

It was J.K. Galbraith who said: 'Meetings are indispensable when you don't want to do anything'. Another saying states that the ideal meeting is two people – with one absent. If there is one thing in business life that is a mixed blessing, then it is surely meetings. Yet so much time is spent in them (and that means they cost a lot), and they *are* an important part of organisational communication, consultation, debate and decision making. We all need them – or certainly we need some of them. You need to work at making yours the positive exceptions. So, at the risk of extending this chapter somewhat, we will investigate the matter in some detail.

We must get the most from them, and we do not need too many of those that are longer than necessary or unconstructive. What is more, good, effective meetings do not just happen. If it is assumed that some deep law of meetings means you must put up with the bad ones in order to get an occasional good one thrown in, then nothing will be done to create a culture of effective meetings. Everyone in an organisation needs actively to work at it. Everybody's role is important, whether they are running a meeting or attending one. Here, we focus on the manager's role when 'in the chair', and start with some of the basics.

The benefits of meetings

Whatever the meeting – large or small, formal or informal, long or short – if it is planned, considered and conducted with an eye on how it can be made to go well, then it can be made to work.

As I have said, we all need some meetings, and their role and importance can vary. Meetings are simply a form of communication, which can be used to:

- inform
- analyse and solve problems
- discuss and exchange views
- inspire and motivate
- counsel and reconcile conflict
- obtain opinion and feedback
- persuade
- train and develop
- reinforce the status quo
- instigate change in knowledge, skills or attitudes.

You can no doubt add to the list. The key role is surely most often to prompt change (there is no point in having a meeting if everything is going to remain the same), and to do that, decisions must be made. And to do that, any meeting has to be constructive and put people in a position where good decisions can prompt appropriate action.

It is also worth noting that good meetings are not just useful, for most people *want* meetings. Having too few can be as big a mistake as having too many. Why do people want them? For various reasons, they believe meetings can (amongst other things):

- keep people informed and up to date
- provide a chance to be heard
- create involvement with others
- are useful social gatherings to allow cross-functional contact
- provide personal visibility and public relations opportunities for the individual
- can broaden experience and prompt learning.

And they are right. Meetings are potentially useful. Indeed, the progress of an organisation can, in a sense, only be certain if meetings are held and if those meetings go well.

Setting up meetings

If a meeting is to be truly successful, then ensuring that success cannot begin only as the meeting starts – the 'I think we're all here, what shall we deal with first?' school of meeting organisation. Making it work starts before the meeting; sometimes a significant period of time before.

First, ask some basic questions, for example:

- Is a meeting really necessary?
- Should it be a regular meeting? (Think very carefully about this one: once a meeting is designated as the weekly (monthly or whatever) such-and-such meeting, it can become a routine that is difficult to break and as such can be an especially easy way to waste time.)
- Who should attend (and who should not)?

If you are clear in your mind in these respects, then you can proceed. Again, avoiding detail here, we can state that some key points to bear in mind are as follows.

- *Setting an agenda*. This is very important, no meeting will go as well if you simply make up the content as you get under way. Notify the agenda in advance and give good notice of contributions required from others.

- *Timing*. Set a start time and a finish time, and then you can judge the way it is to be conducted alongside the duration and even put some rough timing to individual items to be dealt with. Respect the timing too: start on time and try to stick with the duration planned.

- *Objective*. Always set a clear objective so that you can answer the question 'Why is this meeting being held?' (And the answer should never be 'Because it is a month since the last one'!)

- *Prepare yourself*. Read all necessary papers, check all necessary details, and think about how you will handle both your own contribution and the stimulation, and control, of others.

- *Insist others prepare also*. This may mean instilling habits in attendees (for if you pause to go through something that should have been studied before the meeting, then you show that reading beforehand is not really necessary).

- *People*. Who should be there (or not) and what roles individuals should have.

- *Environment*. A meeting will go much more smoothly if people attending are comfortable and if there are no interruptions (so organise switching the coffee pot on and the phones off before you start).

Then, at the appointed hour, you must take charge and make the meeting go well.

Leading a meeting

Even a simple meeting needs someone in the chair. That does *not* imply that whoever is 'in the chair' should be the most senior person present, should do most of the talking or even lead the talking, or that they need to be formally called 'chairperson'. But they should be responsible for *directing* the meeting.

An effectively conducted chairing role can ensure a well-directed meeting, which in turn can mean:

- the meeting will better focus on its objectives
- discussion can be kept more constructive
- a thorough review can be assured before what may otherwise be ad hoc decisions are taken
- all sides of the argument or case can be reflected and balanced
- proceedings can be kept businesslike and less argumentative (even when dealing with contentious issues).

As we can see, all the results of effective chairing are positive and likely to help create an effective meeting. Put succinctly, a good chairperson will lead the meeting, handle the discussion, and act to see objectives are met, with everything occurring promptly, efficiently and effectively. Some of what must be done is simple, and much is common sense; the whole of the role is important.

We will start by referring to two simple but key rules that any chairperson must stick to (and which any group of people meeting should respect). They are, very simply:

1. Only one person may talk at a time
2. The chairperson decides who (should this be necessary).

Already all this should begin to make you think about the qualities of the person who will make a good chairperson. The checklist of responsibilities in Box 6.1 lays out the full picture.

Box 6.1 The meeting leader's responsibilities

The list that follows illustrates the range and nature of the tasks involved. It also shows clearly that there are skills involved – perhaps skills that might usefully be studied, learned and practised.

Whoever is leading the meeting must:

- command the respect of those attending (and if they do not know them, then such respect must be won rapidly by the way they are seen to operate)

- do their homework and come prepared (i.e. having read any relevant documents, taken any other action necessary to help them take charge, and encouraging others to do the same because good preparation makes for more considered and succinct contributions to the meeting)

- be on time

- start on time

- ensure that any administrative matters are organised and will be taken care of appropriately (e.g. refreshments, taking notes or recording minutes)

- start on the right note and lead into the agenda

- introduce people if necessary (and certainly know who's who themselves – name cards can help everyone at some meetings)

- set, and keep to, the rules

- control the discussion, and do so in light of the different kinds of people who may be present – the talkative, the strident, the timid, etc.

- encourage contributions where appropriate or necessary

- ensure everyone has a full chance to contribute

- ask questions to clarify where necessary, for it is important to query anything unclear and do so at once, which can save time and argument – whereas if the meeting runs on with something being misinterpreted, then it will become a muddle and take longer to reach any conclusion

- act to keep the discussion to the point

- listen (as in LISTEN: if the chair has missed things, then the chances of the meeting proceeding smoothly are low and it may deteriorate into 'But you said . . .' types of argument)

- watch the clock, remind others to do the same, and manage the timing and time pressure

- summarise, clearly and succinctly – something that must usually be done regularly

- cope with upsets, outbursts and emotion

- provide the final word, summarising and bringing matters to a conclusion, and similarly linking to any final administrative detail, such as setting the date for the next action or further meeting

- see (afterwards) to any follow-up action, which may be especially important when there is a series of meetings where people promise something at one and turn up at the next having done little or nothing.

And all this must be done with patience, goodwill, good humour and respect for both all those present (and maybe others) and for the objectives of the meeting.

➡ ATTENTION TO DETAIL

Now let us turn to a number of points worth investigating in more detail.

Getting off to a good start

The best meetings start well, continue well and end well. A good start helps set the scene, and this too is the responsibility of whoever is in the chair. It works best to start the meeting in a way that:

- is positive
- makes its purpose (and procedure) clear
- establishes your authority and right to be in charge
- creates the right atmosphere (which may differ if it is to prompt creative thinking or, say, detailed analysis of figures)
- generates interest and enthusiasm for what is to come (yes, even if it is seen as a tedious regular review)
- is immediately perceived as businesslike.

It may also help if the chair involves others early on, rather than beginning with a lengthy monologue – which takes us to the next point.

Prompting discussion

Of course, there are meetings where *prompting* contributions is the least of the problems, but you want contributions from everyone (or why are they there?). So, in order to ensure that you get adequate and representative discussion, and that subsequent decisions are made on all the appropriate facts and information, you may need to prompt discussion.

For example, sometimes there are specific reasons why meeting participants hold back, for example: fear of rejection or ridicule; pressure of other, more senior or more powerful, people; lack of preparation; an incomplete understanding of what has gone before; or, indeed, simply a lack of encouragement to make contributions. A good chairperson will ask for views and do so in a way that prompts open, considered comments.

But note that it is sometimes easy to skew comments (wittingly or not) by the tone or manner with which comments are called for. For instance, a senior manager is unlikely to encourage creative suggestions if he fields his own thoughts first, expressed as: 'It is only a suggestion, but do bear in mind who's making it'. So, do not lead.

Much prompting of comment will come through questions (and the way this is done is important – see also page 35). The other trick is to ensure that you have the measure of different individuals, drawing in, say, the more reticent and acting to keep the overbearing in check. And remember that people may have a variety of motives for the line they take at meetings – some will be more businesslike than others.

Questions must of course be clear. There are two main kinds of question, as stated earlier in Chapter 4 on interviewing, *open* questions and *closed* questions. The particular set of circumstances will affect how questions are best asked – and remember that there is more about this on page 35. Discussion can be prompted around the meeting in more complex ways, and the checklist in Box 6.2 shows six of them.

Box 6.2 Six ways of prompting inputs to discussions

1. *Overhead questions*. These are put to the meeting as a whole, left for whoever picks them up and are useful for starting discussion.

2. *Overhead/directed.* These are put to the whole meeting (as 1) and either followed immediately by the same question to an individual or, after a pause, as a way of overcoming lack of response: 'Now, what do we all think about this? . . . (pause) . . . David?'
3. *Direct to an individual.* Direct to an individual without preliminaries; useful to get an individual reaction or to check understanding.
4. *Rhetorical.* A question demanding no answer can still be a good way to make a point or to prompt thinking, and the chairperson can provide a response if desired. Useful?
5. *Redirected.* This presents a question asked of the chair straight back to the meeting, either as an overhead or direct question: 'Good question. What do we all think? . . . David?'
6. *Developmental question.* This really gets discussion going, it builds on the answer to an earlier question and moves it round the meeting: 'So, Mary thinks it will take too long. Are there any other problems?'

Prompting discussion is as important as control. It is the only way of making sure the meeting is well balanced and takes in all required points of view. If decisions are made in the absence of this, someone may come back to you later saying something like: 'This is not really acceptable, my department never really got a chance to make their case'.

Because of this possibility, it may sometimes be necessary to persevere in order to get all the desired comment that the meeting needs. Ways have to be found to achieve this. One technique is *asking again*, as simple as that: rephrase the question (perhaps it was not understood originally), ensure the point is clear and that people know that a comment *is* required. A second technique is to *use silence*: the trouble is that silence can be embarrassing, but even a short silence to make it clear you will wait for an answer may be sufficient to get someone speaking, so do not rush on, because the point may well deserve a moment's thought.

Concentrating throughout

A well-run, serious meeting demands concentration, and it is the job of whoever is in the chair to assist achieving this by all those present. Concentration is vital, and it needs to be focused on the right things within the meeting. Do not get sidetracked. Beware of running a meeting within a meeting, for sometimes you will unearth separate issues that are worth noting – to be pursued on some *other* occasion.

Beware interruptions. Organise to deal with urgent messages ('Excuse me a moment, I really must deal with this one'), but mobile telephones or simply the refreshments arriving all delay proceedings and hinder concentration. If there are unforeseen interruptions, do not compete with them while people's attention is elsewhere. Wait, deal with them, and then continue, recapping if necessary.

It helps therefore if:

- rules are laid down about messages
- breaks are organised (for longer sessions), so that people know how they can deal with messages, etc. and the meeting sessions are of suitable duration to maintain concentration
- refreshments are organised in advance (or after the meeting)
- others outside the meeting (including switchboard operators and secretaries) are briefed as to how interference matters should be handled. It is as bad for a key customer, say, to be told: 'Sorry, they're in a meeting', as for a meeting to be interrupted; so decide the priorities.

Keeping order

Sometimes even the best-planned and best-organised meeting gets out of hand. So, here it is worth noting some key rules for the chair.

- never get upset or emotional yourself
- pick on one element of what is being expressed and try to isolate and deal with that without heat and to reduce the overall temperature
- agree (at least with the sentiments) before regrouping: 'You are right, this is a damned difficult issue. Emotions are bound to run high. Now, let's take one thing at a time . . .'.

If these approaches do not work, you may have to take more drastic action – for example:

- call for a few minutes complete silence before attempting to move on
- call a short break, and insist it is taken without discussion continuing
- put the problem item on one side until later (though be sure to specify how and when it will be dealt with, and then make sure you do what was agreed)
- abandon the meeting until another time.

This final option is clearly a last resort, but ultimately may be better than allowing disorder to continue. Usually a firm stand made as soon as any sort of unrest occurs will meet the problem head on and deal with it. Whatever happens, DON'T PANIC.

I would not want to give the impression that chairing meetings is all drama, though if discussion never got heated what would that signify? So let us end this section with something more constructive.

Sparking creativity

It is said that managers are not paid to have all the good ideas that are needed to keep their team running effectively, but they *are* paid to make sure there are sufficient ideas to keep it ahead. As a result, many meetings need to be creative. Two heads can really be better than one, even though all too easily new ideas can prompt a tit-for-tat cycle of 'your idea's no good' or 'mine's better' – point-scoring taking precedence over giving the new thinking a chance. This too is something that the chair has to deal with, fostering creative thinking and ensuring that open-mindedness is the order of the day. The chairperson must, therefore:

- actively stimulate creative thinking (saying this is part of the meeting and ruling against instant rejection of ideas without consideration)
- contribute new ideas themselves or steer the discussion into new or unusual directions
- find new ways of looking at things
- consider novel approaches and give them a chance
- aim to solve problems, not tread familiar pathways.

Some groups who meet regularly get better and better at this, but this does not usually happen spontaneously. More often, it is the result of someone putting together the right team and prompting the members to think along certain lines – and, above all, to remain always open-minded.

Now let us conclude by stressing again the influence of choice, role and execution of the chairing task. Without someone at the helm, any meeting risks running onto the rocks.

➡ CREATING AND MAINTAINING A DIALOGUE

Communication between management and staff is a two-way process. If you as a manager want feedback, comment, ideas and suggestions – and you should, because your staff are likely to be far more creative than you think – then you should not just make it possible but positively encourage it.

Some principles and examples illustrate the process. You should encourage communication from staff to you by using the following.

- *Make it expected.* The culture you create within your section, or within the organisation, should be one where two-way communication is an inherent part of what goes on.

- *Stimulate it*, for example by producing regular staff newsletters and similar publications (Note: these can be very useful, but it is easy for them to flag in impact. Beware of setting up such a scheme if you, or whoever undertakes it, cannot sustain the process. Stopping publication may be read as failure, unless something else takes its place.)

- *Make it easy*, with provision for feedback built into communications (for example, with feedback forms being part of various systems in the way that assessment forms are often used after training).

- *React to it.* Acknowledge what people tell you: if it is useful, tell them why and thank them; if it is not, tell them why not and suggest other approaches.

- *Give credit.* If ideas are generated by staff, acknowledge the source, because (in contrast) nothing will ensure that a flow of ideas ceases more quickly than putting them up at other levels as your own.

- *Make time to deal with it*, not least so that your response is seen to be coming from the basis of some consideration.

- *Be available.* Of course you are busy and need to concentrate, but it is death to open and lively communication to say 'I've an open-door policy' and then never to be on the other side of the threshold.

If you involve and use staff effectively, the net result on your own time utilisation should be positive. Make time for people and their contributions will increase efficiency and effectiveness, which in turn should give you more time to concentrate on key issues. Good time management, it should be said, is catching. Set a good example, tell people how you operate (if what you do works!) and the team will be more likely to work at and improve upon their own productivity.

Ensuring continuity

Finally, keep the possibilities for creating a dialogue in mind, find ideas to encourage such a process, and ring the changes to keep people's attention. For example, in one organisation I encountered, in order to stimulate ideas it set up an ongoing programme of 'discussion lunches'. Many people in the section concerned were out of the office a great deal, and often when they were in they worked through their lunch break, eating a sandwich at their desk. So on one (different) day each week a free sandwich lunch was provided for those who had indicated they would attend. The only rule for the group lunch arrangements was that nothing could be discussed except a prescribed topic (chosen through consultation). A secretary took notes and the net result was that focused discussions took place amongst different groups on a regular basis – ideas were generated, problems solved, opportunities identified. What is more, it cost very little and was motivational as well – people liked it.

The whole miscellany of activity that constitutes an organisation's day-to-day activity is a potential basis for communication. Some of it is inherent; some of it (as with the above example) can be created to stimulate and extend the natural process. The manager who takes an active approach to keeping in touch with staff, who makes time for the process and who utilises it systematically and creatively will almost always reap a reward in terms of team performance.

Chapter 7
Training and development

Sending men to war without training is like abandoning them.

(Confucius)

In many organisations, training is often viewed on the one hand as a 'good thing' but on the other as something easily bypassed or postponed in times when cost or other pressures make it inconvenient. In reality, while it may seem to do no harm to sideline training at a particular time, there is a strong case for its not just being a 'good thing' but something for which there is always a need.

➡ THE RATIONALE FOR TRAINING

There is no need here for a long treatise on the merits of training (always a temptation for a trainer!). However, two factors are prime: training is both necessary and desirable.

Training is necessary because, both in the long term and the short term, training needs to be an ongoing part of organisational life and of the management process. This is not so much to act to correct weakness (although this may be a role that is occasionally necessary), but rather to better equip people for changing circumstances. We live in dynamic times. Customer-care staff must be able not only to handle customers in ways that actively build a business, but to operate the computer systems that are usually in front of them as customer calls come in. This is but one example, linked to the IT revolution, amongst many in that area alone; you can doubtless add many more from your own circumstances. Whatever changes come from technology, from the market and competition, or from increasing international changes, there is a continuing need to update and add to people's skills that is unlikely to abate.

Training is also desirable. Here, the rational for training stems more from the people who may be developed. Most people want their jobs to change, they want to tackle new things, and they enjoy the experience both of being able to do new things or do things in new ways and of working in different ways thereafter. Training is essentially motivational and thus, as is commented on elsewhere, has a positive influence beyond its immediate purpose. Organisations with the culture of approving and using training see this reflected in the mood of their people.

Thus training can prompt change. In the short term, it can ensure people are better able to carry out their jobs effectively; in the longer term, staff motivation is likely to be raised by thoughts of long-term career development; and the short- and long-term effects should benefit both the individual and the organisation. The longer-term effect is now especially true, since the events of recent years and the demise of any 'job for life' concept of work have made people look carefully at their own long-term career development.

As with the other topics reviewed throughout this book, we shall concentrate now on how communication affects the training process and the training experience. Ten areas of consideration follow.

➡ TEN STEPS TO TRAINING EFFECTIVENESS

However useful, training is not something that can be applied unthinkingly and expected to work whatever it is and however it takes place. The following are all areas in which communication can assist the training and development process.

Define 'training'

Any manager has as a prime responsibility that of developing the team. The word 'training' has been used in this chapter and there is a danger that this prompts a feeling that training is just attending courses. This is not so. The first thing any manager should do in contemplating this area is to define training *broadly*, because any form of activity that initiates the required changes can be regarded as part of the training and development process.

Of course, such can include course attendance either on public programmes or by setting up tailored in-company programmes – the latter often not only allowing a more specific focus on the needs of the organisation but being more cost-effective also. There is a considerable range encompassed here: attendance may be for a day or a week; it may be in-house or involve time at a business school (here or overseas); or it may encompass other aspects of development than just training, as with a trade conference or exhibition.

But 'training' can also be regarded as including a whole range of other activities, from reading a business book to individual tutorial sessions, from the use of programmed learning or computer-based training to training linked tightly into work projects. Furthermore, the simplest things can often make disproportionately important contributions to team development, and two examples follow.

Many organisations have a 'book of the month' scheme. Every month (or quarter, if you prefer) a business book of some sort is issued to everyone in a group so that they have the common experience of going through the same material. Different topics may sensibly be suggested to different groups, and the frequency can be changed to accommodate topical events. This idea is something that any manager can start at any time – certainly this book is available from the publishers in quantity!

Second, ongoing activities may be able to be linked to training, adding to the development taking place and yet not disrupting operations. One example here, which I have seen in context of the work I do in developing presentational skills, is that of using regular internal meetings to enhance those skills. More than one company has created mandatory practice simply by saying that, for a period, no one may make a major planned input to certain meetings without standing up and doing so in presentational style.

Many examples may add to the process in this kind of way and it pays to be creative about the possibilities.

Linking with appraisal

As Chapter 5 made clear, development and its planning should be an inherent part of the appraisal process. Little more needs to be said here, other than that appraisal (both formal and informal) should act as a significant spur to training. It is from this process that the systems and records linked to training should flow. In some organisations, this can be reasonably formal and linked to other human resources activities such as succession planning; in others, it will be less so.

As a minimum, any manager should have a development sheet for every member of his or her staff. This both records training done but also flags intentions and specific commitments and timings. This will help ensure that matters are not forgotten and that one thing links logically to another. Vague statements such as 'Don't worry, I'll organise something for you on presentation skills soon' can lead to employees being frustrated, because nothing specific appears planned or timed. Personal development is important to many employees, and they can feel neglected and (given the topic used as an example) vulnerable if promised training is not specifically planned – and motivation and management credibility are then compromised. Having things clear, and clearly documented, helps everyone.

Communicating regularly

Communication about development should not just be regular; it should be routine. Development should not be something raised only on special occasions but should be seen as an inherent part of the process of getting things done. Managers need to raise the topic in passing and during meetings on other matters, and they should encourage their staff to do the same. For example, if a project is being discussed and undertaking it will push people into using some new skill, then how requirements can be fitted into planned training and development for the team as the project progresses can logically be part of the project discussion. Certainly, if staff themselves see the need for something, or feel it would be useful in the longer term, then they should feel able to raise it with their manager without waiting extensively, for a quarterly review perhaps, and their experience should be such that such matters are dealt with promptly.

Training has to fit in with broader plans, of course – not least to budgets – and not every suggestion can simply be approved on the simple premise that training is a good thing. 'Six months away at Harvard, no problem' is not the sort of response that should be automatically expected; and sometimes for good reasons (which should be spelt out) the answer to a request for training will be 'No', or 'Not now'. Furthermore, people may need to be shown how to make a persuasive case for training, rather than just request it – but within practical limits you will want a certain amount of well-chosen training discussed, agreed and scheduled to fit in with and support operational activity.

Briefing ahead of the event

Whatever is agreed for a training programme for a member of staff, time should be spent setting it up effectively. This may first involve deciding the nature of the training to be done – attendance on a public programme or linking with others to set up an in-company programme, say. It should certainly involve discussion of:

- the reasons why training is necessary
- the intentions and expectations of what will be done
- the administrative implications (timing, documentation – everything through to how work will be handled while someone is away)
- the debriefing, i.e. what must be done after training in the way of reporting back to the manager.

Even small omissions here can cause problems. I regularly meet people on external courses who have no clear idea what legitimate expenses they may charge on their return to the company. Such details can dilute, if not the training programme's usefulness, then perhaps its motivational impact.

If matters of this sort are thought through, there may be standard documentation that can be originated which eases the task as people are regularly exposed to various training options. For example, the 'Notes for delegates' given in Box 7.1, which I was given by an American consultant and which is quoted in my book *Running an Effective Training Session* (Gower), is a useful statement of how a participant should approach attendance on a formal training programme. It is designed to go in the 'course folder' that participants are provided with at the start of a training course, and it is the sort of thing that can be adapted, developed and given a specific focus within your own company.

Box 7.1 Notes for delegates

1. This manual contains all the basic details of this training programme. Further papers will be distributed during the course so that a complete record will be available by the last session.

2. This is *your* programme. It represents a chance to say what you think – so please do say it. Everyone may learn from such comments and the discussion they prompt.

3. Exchange of experience is as valuable as formal inputs – so listen to what everyone says and try to understand others' point of view.

4. In discussion, support your views with facts, examples or comparisons and stick to the point.

5. Keep questions and comments brief. Do not monopolise the proceedings, but let others have their say so that several points of view are drawn in.

6. Make points as they arise, but remember that participation is an attitude. It includes listening as well as speaking. However, never be afraid to disagree in a constructive way as issues arise.

7. Make notes as the meeting progresses. There is notepaper in the binder for this. It can be particularly useful to note key points from each session, especially aiming for matters that lead to action after the course (when you are bound to be busy as you catch up after an absence). The manual will act as a record, and only you can make sure ideas are implemented and that the catalytic effect of the training course is not wasted.

8. A meeting with colleagues (your manager, your staff, or whoever is appropriate) on your return to day-to-day activities can be valuable and ensure information or instructions can be passed on promptly with a view to action. Schedule this firmly and soon.

9. It will assist everyone if you wear your name badge throughout the programme and stick to the timetable so that there are no delays.

10. Please be sceptical about your own activities and ways of doing things as well as of the course and its content. Only by questioning current practice can new approaches be developed.

Communication at the event

On the assumption that it is a trainer or consultant who is conducting a training event rather than yourself as line manager, it is worth considering what involvement you might have at its commencement. Should you introduce the event, explaining its relevance and demonstrating a commitment to it? Should you attend throughout (especially if you want to be seen as part of the team and as having a need for the same skills)? If not, should you be present at any other time (for example, joining the group for lunch)?

Training, especially formal training held in-company, is certainly an opportunity for this sort of communication. As a consultant who goes into many different organisations in a training role, I am somewhat surprised by how infrequently management at a level above the group attending a course (especially senior management) play any part at all. When they do, however, I am usually impressed. The people who do so seem to have thought it through and concluded that it represents a valuable opportunity.

I remember one general manager, who introduced a course I was conducting and also closed the session. There were then drinks and refreshments laid on and the meeting continued informally. He explained his thinking thus: 'We get together as a group less than I would like. I need to know what people are thinking and I do this [his involvement in the course] because the informal discussion it allows manifestly generates sufficient useful ideas to make it worth the time it takes.' Good thinking.

Debriefing after the event

It should always be a rule for any manager to sit down with people after training; and this applies even to informal training. The opportunity is twofold: it should *prompt action*, and it should *enable evaluation*.

With regard to the first benefit, it should be noted that training can only do three things: impart knowledge, develop skills and change attitudes. After a training session for one of your team, you as manager need to ask whether it has done those three things or not, and make sure it is linked to action. The discussion should be primarily one of allowing a person to report back, with the manager asking questions and only offering guidance if necessary. In this respect it is in the same mould as appraisal – not too much telling. Action points may need teasing out, however, and it may be useful to record them and set a time scale against them. Someone attending, say, a report-writing course may come back with specific intentions, which have a greater chance of taking root if they are linked to specific action. Thus, after the team member next writes a report, the individual should sit down with you and between you should critique it as a further spur to change. Such action needs to be positioned with their and your respective role in it explained, agreed and prevented from becoming intrusive.

Training also needs to be checked in various ways, and this is often linked to an evaluation form. Such a form can be completed at the end of the particular training programme, either immediately or a couple of weeks later to allow digestion to have taken place. In some organisations the evaluation is spread out over time and in two or more stages. If this is linked to constructive discussion, so much the better – again, the emphasis should be on points for future action. One example of how this process can help the manager is by identifying common needs and action, i.e. the experience of one person can be applied elsewhere in the team.

Linking back to appraisal

Any activity and action on the training front needs to link back to the appraisal process. Each such discussion that occurs should relate back to the last. Each discussion updates the last and carries the process forward. Thus the record is important and, as has been said, a clear record should be kept applicable to each employee.

A particular point to note here is continuity. Thus attendance on, say, a report-writing course, may be preceded by reading a good book on the English language and how to use it, and the same course might be followed by a specific project, or indeed another follow-up course. (Note: what is often referred to as 'sandwich' training can be very useful: instead of one long course, the programme is divided into two sections, perhaps additionally with a project acting as a bridge between them.)

In the longer term, it is important that a team member's next appraisal is able to pick up the training element of the review, accurately linking what has gone before to whatever will come next.

Following up (longer term)

Beyond all that has been said so far, there is a need to keep the communication flowing. This can involve the formality of additional meetings or discussions about projects, or it can simply be a comment. For example (continuing the example of training in report writing), if the course has been completed, signed off satisfactorily and (let us be positive) resulted in some changes, then it may be good to find an opportunity to link back to the training on future occasions – even some months ahead. If you were in this position and saw a later (improved) report, then a comment to your team member such as 'This is good, and so much better than what you were doing three months back – the sales director has certainly noticed the change too. He said . . .' can act to:

- motivate (and every easily generated influence here is useful)
- reinforce lessons (a comment can include reminders)
- strengthen habits, so that any newly established practices are that much more likely to continue.

All, or more, of these effects may be possible; all can be useful.

Thus the continuity of training can be sustained and its position maintained as an ongoing part of operational activity, rather than something on the sidelines for when time permits.

A final thought adds to the considerations above. Training needs to be taken seriously. Time needs to be made for it and concentration given to it. The whole way that you approach this as a manager communicates something. At worst, if it is undertaken with less than real commitment, the message may come across that training is not really important – in which case it may be taken as just that.

➡ **AND FINALLY . . .**

Through training and development of your team, you have a major communication opportunity to expand knowledge and capabilities and to extend positive motivation.

Sometimes you have an opportunity to upgrade the whole process. I recently conducted a training programme for a company at a high-quality resort hotel in an attractive overseas location. The arrangements were meticulous. People worked hard during the programme, but it finished at lunchtime on Saturday and people then had the option of staying on for the remainder of the weekend. The breaks and meals were all in a lovely setting and as a result the networking that was encouraged (the group was from around a region) was constructive and took high priority. Such thinking, however it is executed, can be useful.

Training is something that is done to some degree in most organisations. Probably it is usually of some use. Good training, handled with good communications throughout the process, can maximise the learning and the resultant action – and can contribute to the communications culture of the manager and the organisation.

Chapter 8
Consultation and counselling

We must all learn the same way to get round corners.

(Stephen Dando-Collins)

Management presents something of a dichotomy in terms of the way that a manager deals with people. On the one hand, you may well want people to be self-sufficient, just to get on and get the job done; on the other hand, the team is itself a resource and contact with the people is a part of what makes things go better. The fact is that there is clear truth in both views. Staff being self-sufficient in some ways *is* important and does have a direct bearing on productivity. However, this is not the full picture and *working with* staff is important in the following ways, with a participative approach producing a better:

- *transfer of information*, the basis of any kind of understanding or action
- *understanding of the job*, particular tasks and the whole process of work
- *understanding between manager and staff* (which can help them work together more effectively)
- *commitment to the task* and how it will be done
- *a feeling of motivation* about the job and the satisfaction it can bring
- *idea generation*, because two heads often really are better than one.

This means that the management process must necessarily spend time on a variety of forms of interaction and collaboration with staff. One point should be noted here: there is a great deal of difference between consultation and democracy. Communication with staff does not mean that everything that is done must be decided by consensus; though this is a view sometimes taken by staff. Management must manage, and decisions are their province.

Management are not, however, required to do this all on their own in a vacuum. Surely, anything that helps the best decisions to be made and keeps things running smoothly and successfully as a result should be incorporated into the process? This is only common sense – managers are not likely to be all knowing, after all. And the prime resource to help the process is surely the team. Two heads *are* often better than one, and staff who are informed about, and interested in, the department or process concerned are well placed to contribute constructively to getting things right.

The sensible manager regards the team in this way – as an important element of their success.

➡ REGULAR INVOLVEMENT

No constructive dialogue can take place if manager and staff hardly cross paths. To ensure that the frequency and nature of contact necessary takes place, you need to take a conscious approach to it rather than relying on such contacts as events may happen to make necessary.

If you mix the opportunities afforded by the following, then contact can be made to have appropriate substance:

- *Formal group meetings.* There is a danger of overdoing these, especially via weekly (or other-frequency) meetings that become simply a reflex. That said, these are an important part of the interaction. It may be useful to allow some time on occasions for topics that are more general, longer term or simply for idea generation (see the section on 'brainstorming' later in this chapter).

- *One-to-one meetings.* You also need to see each member of your team individually on a regular basis. This is time-consuming and one of the reasons why the span of control of a manager should be restricted – many would regard 7–10 people as the range that any one manager can supervise directly without intervening levels of supervision to share the management load. Some of these sessions will be project-led, linked to the immediate and current workload, whereas others will be linked to appraisal and development or longer-term issues. It is commonly stated by many people about their managers: 'I never see them unless there is a problem'. You need to keep a careful eye on this tendency. If the only contacts you have with an individual staff member are concerned solely with problems, then they will understandably tend to build up a rather resentful view of those meetings – especially if they feel you are jumping on things that they would sort out perfectly well if left alone. Find constructive and future-orientated reasons to meet.

- *Informal meetings*. Principally they should be one-to-one, but sometimes they can be in groups – and sometimes untypical groups. Such informal meetings can contribute practically to the whole process of meeting frequently with staff (and perhaps save time on formal meetings). It is a pity if the sheer pressure of work prohibits such gatherings. It may not seem strictly necessary, but just getting two, three or whatever number of people to break for lunch together and discuss something informally can prove a valuable use of time. I can certainly think of many things in my career that became important, yet started in such a low-key way (including writing books!).

The continuity of all such contacts needs to be borne in mind, as does the involvement of individuals who might find that they seem to be consistently omitted from such gatherings and worry about it. Often a clear sign of management style and competence can be gauged by asking people how often they get together with their manager. If they say, 'Very rarely', 'Only when there's a problem' or 'Not often – thank goodness', this is usually a cause for worry. If they say something like, 'Regularly, but I wish it could be more often', it may well be a sign that contact is felt to be genuinely constructive and useful – because it is.

Consultation

Much of these interaction processes between staff and their manager may be concerned with the gathering of opinions and ideas prior to decisions and action. This is an important process both to undertake and to be seen to undertake. Remember that, as a manager, you are employed to keep your section operating successfully. You are *not* in fact employed to have all the ideas that make this possible, but you *are* employed to see that there are sufficient ideas to do so. The wise manager sees the team as a prime resource in this respect (and we return to just how to prompt creativity in others a little later).

The progression involved in consultation is:

- identifying an opportunity or problem
- spelling out the objectives
- canvassing ideas
- considering these alongside your own, perhaps floating your thoughts about the way forward and obtaining feedback
- making and announcing a decision.

This process is something that must be gone through again and again. Even though the majority view cannot always prevail (the dangers of democracy were mentioned earlier), people are more likely to go along with decisions and action to which they feel their views have contributed. This is an element of what is nowadays called 'ownership'.

➡ SPECIFIC COMMUNICATIONS

As part of the overall process described here, we will investigate three specific areas, both important in themselves and providing examples of the process in action. These are counselling, prompting creativity, and mentoring.

Counselling

Counselling is perhaps best described as the process of 'holding up a mirror to someone so that they can see themselves more clearly'. Often this is problem-related, and it may be that problems dealt with in this way are as much personal as solely work-based. Indeed, some organisations provide a range of counselling services (often buying in advisors from outside) to help employees – and thus prevent time being spent on matters that reduce their effectiveness and productivity. These matters can include routine issues such as financial advice (pensions, mortgages, etc.) and less routine and more difficult ones such as alcoholism or marital problems. The mention of alcoholism (and one could include other issues such as marital problems) make a word of warning appropriate here. Some issues may well tax any manager's knowledge and expertise. There are moments when the *only* route is to involve a professional.

To be successful, counselling demands being done in a way that utilises the following.

- *Respect for the individual.* This in turn demands empathy, or putting yourself in the other person's shoes and seeing – and being seen to see – things from that point of view; with nothing censorious being introduced. You will hardly endear the counselling process to someone if you begin by giving them the impression that the matter is silly, unimportant or the individual's own fault.

- *Appropriate confidentiality.* People clearly need the confidence of knowing that you will not immediately tell everyone else about their situation. This confidence needs to be in the process and in you individually.

- *Careful questioning.* This really gives people an opportunity to talk, perhaps about things they find awkward or embarrassing and would rather leave unsaid. Without the full picture, however, the session may be less than helpful – so, points may need to be delicately pursued even when the person dries up: 'It made me really angry . . .' (silence) 'Angry? How did you feel?' This kind of questioning reflects back the thought and acts to allow it to be explained further.

- *Listening.* This is always important in communications (see page 36), and never more so than with counselling.

- *A focused approach.* You must ensure that the session stays on target. Test understanding if necessary and evaluate the messages you receive as you go (reading between the lines), so that any resolution of a problem is based on the full and correct facts of the matter.

- *An impartial and unemotive approach*. You must stay detached and objective and always be seen to do so.

Advice and resolution from such sessions may as likely come from the person themselves being led to see things differently and more clearly, as from straight advice along the lines of 'I think you should do so and so'. Indeed, advice should always be dispensed with care.

Prompting creativity

People are often innately creative – given the opportunity. This may be no more than asking 'What do you think? . . . Any ideas?', but it is important that the attitude of the manager in this way is understood; and that a feeling of confidence is cultivated in people that they *can be* creative. If they are never asked or consulted, they may come to believe that this is because they really do have nothing to offer. Sometimes a long-term 'campaign' is necessary to build confidence in individual team members, and this can be an important thread in keeping in touch with and involving staff.

Two specific approaches here illustrate the concept in different ways: the creative 'magic formula' and 'brainstorming'.

The creative 'magic formula'

This is a method of generating thinking (and saving yourself time while developing others), the deployment of which is literally invaluable.

Imagine: a head comes round your door and someone says, 'I'm not sure about this, can you spare a moment to go through it?' As a caring manager you clear a few minutes (then or later). As a busy manager you may be tempted to focus primarily on minimising the interruption. You look or listen and respond with a quick comment, often virtually an instruction, to 'do it this way'. A better response throws it straight back to the staff member: 'What do you think makes sense here?' or similar being the comment intended to get people thinking. The individual may ask for time, or discussion may continue there and then as the team member perhaps poses some alternatives. You can then insist, 'Fine, but what makes best sense in this instance?' Your consistent use of this approach will quickly become recognised.

People, gradually understanding that you are not going to give them an instant answer, will give some thought to the problem first, though they may still check it out with you. Variations are possible. You might respond to such a question by getting two staff members into constructive discussion, 'Have a word with John and let me know what you work out' (perhaps identifying why John, or whoever, is suitable). This process, which can develop into a short meeting, may take a little longer than an instant 'do this' response, but it will:

- save time in the longer term by developing the right habits
- develop self-sufficiency (for witness how people usually make the right decision when you are not there to ask and they have to act alone)
- spur creative thinking and new ideas, either by the individual concerned or through the discussion with you or others.

Brainstorming
Brainstorming is a group activity and can be used to provide an almost instant burst of idea generation. It needs a prescribed approach, as follows.

- Gather people around and explain the objectives.
- Explain that there are to be no comments on ideas at this stage.
- Allow a little time for thought (singly or, say, in pairs).
- Start taking contributions and noting them down (publicly on, say, a flipchart).
- When a good-sized list is established, begin analysis of it.
- Group similar ideas together, if necessary, to make the list more manageable.
- Review the list in open-minded discussion.
- Identify ideas that can be taken forward.

Such a session must exclude the word 'impossible' from the conversation, at least initially and especially when used in senses such as 'It's impossible, we don't do things that way' (why not?) or 'It's impossible, we tried it and it didn't work' (how long ago and in what form?).

By avoiding negative or censorious first responses, and by allowing one idea to spark another and variations on a theme to refine a point (perhaps taking it from a wild idea to something practical), you may well be able to produce a genuinely new approach. It can be fun to do, satisfying in outcome and time-efficient to undertake – and a group who brainstorms regularly get better at it, and quicker and more certain in their production of good, usable ideas.

Try it, and you might be surprised at the results.

Mentoring

The role of mentor is a practical one. It is perhaps best thought of from the receiving end. What kind of ongoing help and advice do people want? The best simple interpretation of what a mentor does is that of a 'sounding board', combined with an element of cajoling.

The first necessity is that people feel free – indeed encouraged – to come to you to put you in this role. What is necessary is:

- a trusting relationship
- the ability for constructive criticism to be exchanged and built on
- the open sharing of problems
- objectivity.

Also, of course, there must be a willingness to set aside the time that is taken in such discussions. The activity here can vary enormously. It consists as much of a member of your staff knowing that they can lift the telephone and have 60 seconds of your time for a quick comment on something, as of the formality of sitting down and going through something in more detail.

The key to a successful mentoring relationship is continuity. Sessions should build one on another, becoming more constructive and more useful (and perhaps less time-consuming as people get to know one another, and the process they are involved with, better). In many ways it is an inherent part of any good manager–subordinate relationship; if according it the formality of the 'mentoring' name makes it more certain to happen and be constructive, so be it.

Mentoring is a two-way process. Any manager who has drawn benefit from a mentor during his or her own life – as I certainly have been lucky enough to do (though I have unashamedly encouraged the process) – will need little persuasion of the benefits of including it as a tangible part of the relationship with the team.

➡ SUMMARY OF THE CHAPTER

The whole emphasis of the comment here has been twofold: first, to show the advisory nature of much of the communication between management and staff; and, second, to show the need for a style of communication that accommodates it. This is not to support people in the negative sense of their not being able to cope on their own. It is additive. It allows the building of strengths and injects fresh thinking into everything that is done.

Making this aspect of communication constructive is one of the most useful things a manager can do when working with the team. Consultation and counselling are generally appreciated by staff, they act positively and the results link directly to those that will be achieved in operational terms by the team.

Chapter 9
An element of motivation

When the chips are down, anyone with any get-up-and-go gets up and goes.

(Anon)

Motivation matters. There is considerable research to show that people who are (to put it simply) happy in their work will perform better than those who are not. As the job of the manager is about getting results *through* other people, rather than for them, the motivational state is important. In terms of both productivity and quality of action, maximising motivational feeling will assist performance. Similarly, it is easy for any dilution of motivation to act to reduce performance – something that ultimately reflects on the manager. Multiply the effects, either positive or negative, by the number of people reporting to you and you see the real importance of good motivation.

So, managers must act not just to ensure that people perform well, but also to ensure that they do so consistently and reliably. Good motivation also acts to help make sure that people are as self-sufficient as possible, are able to make decisions – good decisions – on their own, and can take action to keep things running smoothly. If you have to check every tiny detail and give moment-by-moment instructions, then neither productivity nor the quality achieved are likely to be as good as they might be. There is every difference in the world between people being able to do something and do it well, however, and being *willing* to do it and do it well.

Thus managers need to motivate people, rather than leave them to their own devices. Motivation, like so much else in management, does not just happen. It must be recognised as an active process – one that you need to allow some time for on a continuing basis.

➡ HOW MOTIVATION WORKS

The theory of motivation is extensive and this is not the place to do otherwise than recap some essential principles. If you are entirely familiar with the principles, then by all means skip to the next main heading.

A basis for successful motivation

Many people took the view in years gone by that getting performance from staff was a straightforward process. You told them what to do and they did it; period. And if that was, for some reason, insufficient, then it was backed by the power of management; effectively by coercion.

Management by fear still exists. In any economy with less than full employment, the ultimate threat is being out of a job. But whether the threat is subtle or specific, whether it is just an exaggerated form of arm twisting or out-and-out bullying, even if it works (at least in the short term) it is resented. The resentment factor is considerable. People fight against anything they consider to be an unreasonable demand; so much so that the fighting may tie up a fair amount of time and effort, with performance ending up as only the minimum that people 'think they can get away with'.

Your job as a manager, in contrast, is not simply to get things done but to get things done *willingly*. Only if people want to do things and are encouraged to do things well can they be relied on actually to do them really well. Motivation provides reasons for people to want to deliver good performance.

If this sounds like no more than common sense, then that is because it is. For example, are you more likely to read on if I tell you that if you do not I will come round to your house and break all your windows, or if I persuade you that you will find doing so really useful and offer you some sort of tangible reward? (I do intend that you will find it useful, incidentally, but sadly there is no free holiday on offer.) Motivation works because it reflects something about human nature, and understanding the various theories about this is a useful prerequisite to deploying motivational techniques and influencing staff behaviour.

'Theory X' and 'Theory Y'

The first of the classic motivational theories that is worthy of some note was documented by Douglas McGregor. He defined the human behaviour relevant to organisational life in terms of 'Theory X' and 'Theory Y'.

'Theory X' makes the assumption that people are lazy, uninterested in work or responsibility. They must thus be pushed and cajoled to get anything done in a disciplined way, with reward assisting the process to some degree. 'Theory Y' takes the opposite view; it assumes people want to work. They enjoy achievement, gain satisfaction from responsibility and are naturally inclined to seek ways of making work a positive experience.

There is truth in both pictures. What McGregor was doing was describing extreme positions. Of course, there are jobs that are inherently boring and mundane, and others that are obviously more interesting; and it is no surprise that it is easier to motivate those doing the latter. Even so, it is a matter of perspective. There is an old, apocryphal story of a despondent group of convicts breaking rocks being asked about their feelings concerning the backbreaking work. All expressed negative feelings, except one, who said simply 'It makes it bearable if I keep the end result in mind – I'm helping to build a cathedral'.

Whether you favour Theory X or Theory Y – and Theory Y is surely more attractive – it is suggested that motivation creates a process that draws the best from any situation. Some motivation can help move people from a Theory X situation to a Theory Y one. Thereafter it is easier to build on positive Theory Y principles to achieve still better motivational feelings and still better performance; and your communication should reflect this fact.

Maslow's hierarchy of needs

Another theory that helps describe the basic situation on which all motivational effort must be directed is that of Abraham Maslow. He wrote that people's needs were satisfied progressively. In other words, only when basic needs are met do their aspirations rise and are other goals set.

The first such needs are psychological: enough to eat and drink, warmth, shelter and rest. In a working environment people need to earn sufficient to buy the answers to these. Next come needs of safety and protection: ranging from job security (one that is less easily met than once was the case) to good health (with the provision of healthcare schemes by employers now very common).

Beyond that he described social needs: all those associated with working in groups and with people. The work environment is a social environment; indeed, for some people, contacts formed through work may represent the majority of the personal relationships in their lives. Linked to these are a further level of needs such as recognition within the organisation and amongst the people comprising the work environment, and the ability to feel self-confidence, self-fulfilment and a positive outlook to a better future – one in which we are closer to realising our perceived potential and happier because of it.

However this theory is defined and described, it is the hierarchical nature of it that is most important. What it says, again wholly sensibly, is that people's motivations can only be satisfied if this hierarchy is respected. For instance, it suggests that motivational input is doomed to be ineffective if it is directed at one level when a lower level is unsatisfied. It is thus little use to tell people how satisfying a job is if they are consumed with the thought that the low rate of pay makes them unable to afford basic essentials. Thus all communication with staff designed to have a motivational impact must bear in mind the whole picture.

Again, this does not describe the whole process in a way that you can use as it stands to create the right motivation in your office, but it helps show one element of what is involved.

Hertzberg's motivator/hygiene factors

This third theory leads to a view of the process that links much more directly to an action-based approach to creating positive motivation. Hertzberg described two categories of factor: first, the hygiene factors – those dissatisfiers that switch people off if they cause difficulty; and, second, the motivators – factors that can make people feel good. Let us consider these in turn.

The dissatisfiers (or hygiene factors)
These factors Hertzberg listed, in order of their impact (the most important appearing first), as follows:

- company policy and administrative processes
- supervision
- working conditions
- salary
- relationship with peers
- personal life (and the impact of work on it)
- status
- security.

All are external factors that affect the individual, and because of this they are sometimes referred to as 'environmental' factors. When things are without problem in these areas, all is well motivationally; if there are problems, they all contain considerable potential for diluting any positive motivational feeling.

Note, in case perhaps it surprises you, that salary appears in this list. It is a potential dissatisfier. Would you fail to raise your hand in answer to the question: 'Would you like to earn more money?' Most people would certainly say 'yes'. At a particular moment, an existing salary may be acceptable (or unacceptable), but it is unlikely to turn you on and be a noticeable part of your motivation. So too for those who work for you – but more of this later.

It is issues in the listed areas that give rise to gripes and to a feeling of dissatisfaction that rumbles on. If the firm's parking scheme fails to work and you always find someone else in your place – perhaps someone more senior whom it is difficult to dislodge – it rankles and the feeling is always with you. There are therefore, as we shall see later, many things springing from these areas for managers to work at, where getting them right can make a positive contribution to boosting the motivational climate of the team.

The restriction here is that these things are not those that can add powerfully to positive motivational feeling. Get things right here and demotivation is avoided. To add more, you have to turn to Hertzberg's second list.

The satisfiers (or motivators)
Hertzberg proposed that these define the key factors that create positive motivation. They are, in order of relative power:

- achievement
- recognition

- the work itself
- responsibility
- advancement
- growth.

It is all these factors, stemming from the intrinsic qualities of human nature, that offer the best chance of being used by management to play their part in ensuring that people want to perform and perform well. Communication is a vital part of this picture. Every piece of communication can (and probably will) have motivational overtones. For example, put in a new system that requires people to fill in a new form on a regular basis and – if it is not made clear why it is useful – people will be demotivated because it relates to the list of dissatisfiers – specifically, policy and administration.

Similarly, a wealth of communications affects the motivational climate, jogging the overall measure of it one way or the other. For example:

- *job descriptions, clear guidelines and adequate training* all give a feeling of security, without which motivation suffers
- *incentives* will work less effectively if their details are not clearly communicated (for instance, an incentive payment scheme may be allowed to seem so complicated that no one works out how they are doing and motivation suffers as a result)
- *routine jobs* can be made more palatable by communicating to people what an important contribution they make
- *job titles* may sensibly be chosen with an eye on how they affect people's feelings of status as well as a description of function ('sales executive' may be fine and clear to customers, but most prefer titles like 'account service manager').

Furthermore, the same essential act can be changed radically in terms of the effect it has motivationally just by varying the way in which communication occurs. For example, the simplest and least expensive positive motivational act a manager can engage in is probably uttering the simple phrase 'Well done' (and which of us can put a hand on our heart and say we do even that sufficiently often? ... But I digress). Consider some different ways of doing that, listed in what is probably an ascending order of motivational power:

- saying well done, one to one
- saying it in public, in an open-plan office
- saving it to be said at an 'occasion' (anything from a departmental meeting to a group taking a coffee break together)
- saying it (in one of the ways listed) and then confirming it in writing
- getting the initial statement (however it may be done) endorsed by someone senior
- publishing it in a company newsletter.

The implications here are clear. Not only is motivation itself primarily executed through communication, but the precise form of that communication needs to be borne in mind so that it contributes directly to the effect achieved. Sometimes the opportunity to motivate and do so successfully is dependent mostly on the way things are communicated. The case described in Box 9.1 – a situation that I was involved in a while ago – reinforces this point.

Box 9.1 Big problem, small problem

A travel agency is essentially a service and people business. In one particular firm, with a chain of some 30 retail outlets across several counties of the UK, business was lagging behind targets. The industry was, at the time, not in recession; rather, the lag was due to competitive activity and was potentially something that a more active, sales-orientated approach could cure. Initially the approach to the problem was to draw attention to the problem at every level. Memos were circulated to all staff. The published figures – the sales revenue planned for the business, the amount coming from holidays, flights, etc. – were substantial, and even the shortfall was some hundreds of thousands of pounds.

The result? Well, certainly the sales graph did not turn upwards. But, equally clearly, morale dropped. People went from feeling they worked for a successful organisation to thinking it was – at worst – foundering; and the staff felt that the fault was being laid at their door. The figures meant little to the kind of young people who manned the counters – they were just unimaginably large numbers to which they were wholly unable to relate personally.

With a sales conference coming, a different strategy was planned. The large shortfall was amortised and presented as a series of smaller figures – one per branch. These 'catch-up' figures were linked to what needed to be sold, in addition to normal business, in order to catch up and hit target. It amounted, if I remember rightly, to two additional holidays (2 adults and 2.2 children) per branch per week. Not only was this something staff could easily relate to, but it was something they understood and felt was possible. Individual targets, ongoing communication to report progress and some prizes for branches hitting and besting these targets in a number of ways completed the picture.

The result this time? The numbers slowly climbed. The gap closed. Motivation increased with success in sight. And a difficult year ended with the company hitting the original planned targets – and motivation continued to run high as a real feeling of achievement was felt.

The key here was, I am sure, one of communications. The numbers and the difficulty of hitting them did not change. The perception of the problem, however, was made manageable, personal and – above all – was made to seem achievable. The results then showed that success was possible. No significant costs were involved here, just a little thought and time to make sure that the communications were right, that motivation was positively affected and that results stood a real chance of rising.

As a last thought about this example, it should be said that while the difficulties that were surmounted by the travel company make it a good example, the same principles apply to *positive* situations. It is as important, and often easier, to build on success as to tackle difficulties. Indeed, this may produce the greatest return for the action taken. But this is only the case if the communication with people is clear, and messages are put in a way that makes them easy to relate to.

➡ KEY SUCCESS FACTORS

It may seem from what has been said already that motivation is a complex business. To some extent this is so. Certainly, it is a process affected by many, and disparate, factors. The list of factors affecting motivation, for good or ill, may be long; and that is where any complexity lies. But the process of linking to them in terms of action is often straightforward.

The very nature of people, and how their motivation can be influenced suggests five important principles for the manager dedicated to actively motivating people. These are:

1. There is no magic formula.
2. Success is in the detail.
3. Continuity
4. Timing
5. Bear others in mind.

Each of the five is described a little further below.

There is no magic formula

No one thing, least of all money, provides an easy option to creating positive motivation at a stroke, and anything that suggests itself as such a panacea should be viewed with suspicion.

Success is in the detail

Good motivation comes from minimising the factors that tend to create dissatisfaction and maximising the effect of those factors that can create positive motivation. *All of them*, in both categories, must be considered; it is a process of leaving no stone unturned, with all those found able to contribute to the overall picture being useful.

What is described as the motivational climate of an organisation, department or office is the sum of all the pluses and minuses in terms of how individual factors weigh in the balance. And communication plays a key role.

Continuity

The analogy of climate is a good one. As a small-scale example of this, bear in mind a glasshouse. Many factors contribute to the temperature inside. Heating, windows, window blinds, whether a door or window is open, whether the heating is switched on, and so on. But some such things – whatever they are – are in place and contributing to the prevailing temperature *all the time.*

So too with motivation. Managers must accept that creating and maintaining a good motivational climate takes some time and is a continuous task. Anything – perhaps everything – they do can have motivational side-effects. For example, as was mentioned, a change of policy may involve a new system and its use may have desirable effects (for instance, saving money), but if complying with the system is seen as bureaucratic and time-consuming the motivational effect may be negative despite results being changed for the better.

Overall, the trick is to spend the minimum amount of time in such a way that it secures the maximum positive effect.

Timing

Another thing that must be recognised is the differing time scales involved here.

Signs of low motivation can be a good early warning of performance in peril. If you keep your ear to the ground you may be able to prevent negative shifts in performance or productivity by letting signs of demotivation alert you to the coming problem. The level of motivation falls first, and performance follows.

Similarly, watch for the signs after you have taken action aimed at actively affecting motivation positively. Performance may take a moment to start to change for the better, but you may well be able to identify that this is likely through the signs of motivation improving. Overreacting because things do not change instantly may do more harm than good. If motivation is improving, performance improvement is usually not far behind.

So, the timing of communication is vital too. A busy moment and something allowed to go by default may lead to problems at some point in the future.

Bear others in mind

There is a major danger in taking a censorious view of any motivational factor, either positive or negative. Most managers find that some at least of the things that worry their staff, or switch them on, are not things that would affect themselves. No matter; it is the other people who matter. If you regularly find things that you are inclined to dismiss as not of any significance, be careful. What matters to you is *not* the same as what matters to others.

If you discover something that can act towards you influencing your people, however weird or trivial it may seem, use it. Dismissing it out of hand – and in communications terms, failing to explain something adequately just because it is not something that you feel is important – will simply remove one factor that might help influence the motivational climate. It will make achieving what you want just a little more difficult. At worst, it will also result in your being seen as uncaring.

A further aspect of motivation now needs to be added, namely that concerned specifically with involving people.

➡ INVOLVEMENT AND EMPOWERMENT

The word 'empowerment' enjoyed a brief vogue in the mid-1990s, as one of a succession of management fads that, if you believe the hype, solve all problems and guarantee to put any organisation on the road to success. If only! On the other hand, there is sense in the idea of empowerment. It may not solve everything, but it is a useful concept and it does provide additional bite to the prevailing motivational feeling.

Empowerment in action

Rather than describe leaden definitions, let us start with an example. The Ritz-Carlton have enjoyed good publicity not only for the undoubted quality of their many hotels, but for a particular policy they operate. Say you are staying in one of their hotels and have (perish the thought) something to complain about. So, reeling from the stench from your minibar or whatever, you stick your head out of your room door into the corridor and take up the matter with a passing chambermaid.

Now, whoever you were to speak to, the procedure would be the same. *Every* single member of the hotel's staff is briefed to be able to handle your complaint. They do not have to find a supervisor, check with the manager or thumb through the rule book. They sort it. As they think fit. And they have a budget to do so: every single member of staff can spend so many dollars (I think it started as $500, but has no doubt changed) instantly, and without any checks, to satisfy a guest's complaint.

So, to continue our example, if the minibar was dirty they could summon someone to clean it at once (even if that meant paying overtime), refill it with complimentary drinks and throw in a free bottle of fine wine and a bowl of fruit on a side table to make up to the guest for the inconvenience.

Such staff are empowered.

It is an approach that gets things done. It regards staff as a key resource, not only one to get tasks completed but one that can, in many ways, decide just how they get it done. The empowerment approach goes way beyond simple delegation and plays on the appeal of responsibility to the individual to get things done and done right. It works in part because staff like it. Being empowered is motivational.

Behind empowerment

Empowerment does not allow managers, however, to abrogate their responsibility, nor does it represent anarchy, a free-for-all where anything goes. The chambermaid (in our example mentioned above) does not have the right to do just anything, only to select, or invent, something that will meet the customer's needs and that does not cost more than the budget to implement.

Staying with our hotel example, consider what must lie in the background. Staff must:

- *understand guests*, their expectations and their likely reaction to difficulties (and how that might be compounded by circumstances – having to check out quickly to catch a flight, for example)
- *be proficient at handling complaints* so as to deal promptly, politely and efficiently with anything that might occur
- *have in mind typical solutions* and be able to improvise to produce better or more appropriate solutions to match the customer situation

- *know the system*: what cost limit exists, what documentation needs completing afterwards, who needs to be communicated with, etc.

The systems aspect is, however, minimal. There is no need for forms to be filled in in advance, no hierarchy of supervisors to perform checks, and most of what must happen is left to the discretion of the individual members of staff.

The essence of such empowerment is a combination of self-sufficiency and a solid foundation of training and management practices that ensure that staff will be able to do the right thing.

Letting go

Often, when I conduct training courses, the room is full of managers tied, as if by an umbilical cord, to their mobile telephones or pagers. Many of the calls that are made in the breaks are not responses to messages, they are just to 'see everything is all right'. Are such calls, or the vast majority of them, really necessary? I wonder.

The opposite of this situation is more instructive. See if this rings a bell. You get back to the office after a gap (a business trip, a holiday, whatever). Everything seems to be in order. When you examine some of the things that have been done you find that your view is that staff have made exactly the right decisions, yet . . . you know that *if you had been in the office, they would have asked you about some of the issues involved.* Some of the time staff empower themselves, and when they do, what they do is very often right.

All empowerment does is put this kind of process on a formal footing. It creates more self-reliant staff, able to consider what to do, make appropriate decisions and execute the necessary action successfully. Perhaps we should all allow this to happen more often and more easily.

Making empowerment possible

Empowerment cannot be seen as an isolated process. It is difficult to view it other than as an integral part of the overall management process.

You can only set out to create a feeling of empowerment by

utilising a range of other specific management processes to that end, although the process perhaps starts with attitude and communication. What degree of autonomy do your staff feel you allow them? If they feel restricted and, at worst, under control every moment of the day, they will tend to perform less well. Allowing such feeling to exist is certainly a good way to stifle initiative and creativity.

So you need to let it be known that you expect a high degree of self-sufficiency and to manage in a way that makes that possible. All sorts of items contribute to this approach, but the following – all aspects of communication – are certainly key:

- *A clear policy.* Empowerment will only ever work if everyone understands the intentions of the organisation (or department) and its role (via clear job descriptions) so as to allow the group to put into context any action that may need to be decided upon. The other requirement of an empowered group is an absence of detailed rules to be followed slavishly, but clear guidelines about the results to be aimed at.

- *Clarity of communication.* This feature has been mentioned before, but it is especially important in the context of motivation. Any organisation can easily be stifled by lack of, or lack of clarity in, communication. An empowered group is doubly affected by this failing.

- *Little interference.* Management must set things up so that people can be self-sufficient, and then keep largely clear. Developing the habit of taking the initiative is quickly stifled if staff know nothing they do will be able to be completed without endless checks (mostly, they will feel, made just at the wrong moment).

- *Consultation.* A management style in which consultation is inherent acts as the best foundation for an empowered way of operating. It means that the framework within which people take responsibility is not simply wished, perhaps seemingly unthinkingly, upon them but is something that they helped to define – and of which they have taken ownership.

- *Feedback.* Empowerment needs to maintain itself, actions taken must not sink into a rut and cease to be appropriate because time has passed, and no one has considered the implications of change. Feedback may only be a manifestation of consultation, but some controls are also necessary. Certainly the overall ethos must be one of dynamism, continuing to search for better and better ways to do things as a response to external changes in an even more dynamic and competitive world.

- *Development.* It is axiomatic that if people are to be empowered, they must be competent to execute the tasks required of them and do so well. This ties in with what was said about training and development in Chapter 7.

An enlightened attitude to development is motivational. A well trained team of people are better able to be empowered, as well as having the confidence and the skills. An empowered and competent team is more likely to generate better productivity and performance. It is a virtuous circle.

Most of the time the answer is in the manager's hands. Keep too tight a reign on the team and it will no doubt perform but may lack the enthusiasm to excel. Management should have nothing less than excellence of performance as its aim, for market pressures mean that any other view risks the organisation being vulnerable to events and competitive action. Alternatively, too little control, which amounts to an abrogation of responsibility, also creates risk. In this case, staff will fly off at a tangent, losing sight of their objectives and, at worst, do more than what takes their fancy.

Like so much else, a balance is necessary. Empowerment is not a panacea, but an element of this philosophy can enhance the performance of most teams. Achievement and responsibility rank high as positive motivators, and empowerment embodies both. Motivation will always remain a matter of detail, with management seeking to obtain the most powerful cumulative impact from the sum total of their actions, while keeping the time and cost of so doing within sensible bounds.

Empowerment is one more weapon in the armoury of potential techniques available to you, but it is an important one. Incorporate it in what becomes the right mix of ideas and methods for you, your organisation and your team, make it clear to people how you operate, and it can help make the whole team work effectively.

The ten keys to motivational success

The following ten keys to adopting a motivational style summarise what I have described so far in this chapter and what ought to create success:

1. always think about the people aspects of everything
2. keep a list of possible motivational actions, large and small, in mind
3. monitor the 'motivational temperature' regularly
4. see the process as continuous and cumulative
5. ring the changes in terms of method to maintain interest
6. do not be censorious about what motivates others, either positively or negatively
7. beware of panaceas and easy options
8. make sufficient time for it
9. evaluate what works best within your group
10. remember that, in part at least, there should be a 'fun' aspect to work.

Make motivating, and the communication that transmits it, a habit. Take a creative approach to it and you may be surprised by what you can achieve. The motivation for you to motivate others is in the results.

➡ AIMING FOR EXCELLENCE

Finally in this chapter, remember that even the best performance can often be improved. Motivation is not simply about ensuring that what should happen happens. It is about striving – and achieving – excellence. All sorts of features contribute, from the original calibre of the staff you recruit to the training you give them, but motivation may be the final spur that creates exceptional performance where it would otherwise only be satisfactory.

It is an effect worth seeking; and it is one multiplied by the number of staff involved. How much more can be achieved by 10, 20 or more people all trying just that bit harder, than can be by one manager, however well intentioned? Motivation makes a real difference.

Chapter 10
Conflict and control

When people are least sure, they are often most dogmatic.

Nice though it might be, groups of people do not always work amicably together. Sometimes there is friction. This can be constructive, where it can prompt argument – discussion – and the process of ideas and counter-ideas being thrown to and fro and can therefore result in useful outcomes – perhaps outcomes that would not have occurred otherwise.

But situations occur where conflict overpowers sensible dialogue and argument, and sometimes negative feelings and emotion take over. Then the outcome can be anything but amicable or constructive. What causes this?

It may be a whole range of influences. Perhaps something unreasonable has happened, or perhaps the people involved just dislike each other. But the conflict may be evidence of a focus on personalities (rather than action), on face-saving, on the preservation of power or a need to 'get back at people' for some real or imaginary upset or unfairness. It is human nature. It will happen even in the best-managed group, but it needs to be dealt with.

➡ DEALING WITH CONFLICT

The manager has the role of peacemaker in conflict situations. Faced with conflict between members of your team (or with others elsewhere in the organisation – perhaps another department), you as manager responsible for sorting it out must:

- get to the root of the problem

- keep calm and in control at all times
- deal with things impartially
- lay down clear rules of acceptable behaviour
- deal with matters through discussion, not argument.

The processes and approaches involved then include:

- giving the matter adequate time – for example, it may be necessary to see people separately first and important for such meetings to allow equal time each (which will be read as fairness)
- listening, and being seen to listen, carefully (see page 35)
- investigating and dealing with matters in context of your underlying belief in the people concerned
- aiming to build bridges that will lead people away from conflict rather than, perhaps unrealistically, attempting to magic problems away instantly
- being careful to remain uncensorious about matters – matters that could seem silly to you, but seem overwhelmingly important to others.

Resolving conflict

Conflict often starts small but gradually builds into something major. Small differences of opinion may start the process, but then conflict escalates as people become defensive, aggressive or sometimes malicious. By the time it is clear that something must be sorted out, positions are entrenched and it has become as much a battle of wills as a tangible problem.

Even so, discussion is the route out. As stated above, it may help to see different people separately first to get their view uninterrupted by argument. Then both, or all, parties need to sit down together and discuss the matter. Such a session calls for strong chairmanship (see pages 72–75), and needs clear rules – for example only one person talking at a time, no interruptions, no insults (stick to the facts). You need to listen, make notes and recap regularly to be sure that everyone is moving forward together. Your calm businesslike manner should help you to keep order and make it clear that the only route to resolution is a rational one.

The heat has to be taken out of situations, and this may mean curtailing argument and reconvening when tempers have calmed. Most people are embarrassed by conflict – both theirs and other people's (for it is uncomfortable being on the sidelines of others' arguments, especially if invited to take sides). Ultimately, therefore, people ought to be expected to return to more rational ways of dealing with matters, and your guidance and role as peacemaker must encourage this.

People may have to agree to differ in some respects, but misunderstandings should have been ironed out and the need to work amicably together must be shown to override what may come to be seen as unimportant petty squabbling. People must reach a fresh point where they can work together. Transient problems can usually be resolved. Realistically, occasionally you may need to take action that removes a relationship that manifestly has no hope of existing peacefully and constructively, which might be done by reorganisation, or could – if someone's behaviour warrants it – result in dismissal. Clear rules of expected behaviour, however, should ensure that matters rarely get to a really difficult stage.

There is merit in being seen as firm in sticking to such rules (which can be informal yet given weight), sensitive in handling matters of conflict, yet focused on ensuring the belief that the prime objective is action to ensure work is completed satisfactorily.

➡ DISCIPLINARY ACTION

Every organisation has rules: about getting to work on time, dress code, claiming expenses, reporting procedures and a host of other topics. Within this context, the first essential is to make sure that everyone knows what the rules are and, sensibly, why they exist. This might need some documentation, and many organisations have operating manuals, or similar documentation, that spell out requirements for each of its departments. The second essential is that you consistently deal with matters in a way that is seen to be fair.

Sometimes staff behave in a way that demands firm remedial action. At worst this could involve a breach of the law, where someone is suspected of stealing or – generally more likely – of transgressing an element of employment law. More often the transgression is less severe, but such events can still be disruptive, they can lead to a breakdown of order within the workplace, and they need firm and appropriate handling.

There are two forms of possible action in response to a disciplinary situation: informal and formal.

Informal disciplining

An example makes the point about informal handling of things where, provided the reason for a rule that has been broken is clear, no hassle will be tolerated.

Consider a reporting system, one for example designed to note the customer calls made by members of a field sales team. Getting the information in, on time, at the end of each month is important. One person being late can prevent the total figures being analysed and used. Chasing up that person – or, worse, several of them – wastes time unnecessarily and generally there are better things to do with one's time. You can do worse than say so: 'If I am going to be able to consult on important matters, we have to have other things that work like clockwork, are not constantly questioned, and on which no time is wasted'. Then if someone is late, sanctions must be clear, immediate and practical.

In more than one company I know, such systems are linked to the payment of expenses. Unless every report form for the month is in on time, complete and legible, the expenses claim (which usually is on time!) is deferred for a month. It acts as a control and sends a reasonable message designed to influence not just the completion of a single form but attitudes to this sort of system and rule. When they think about it, people do recognise the balance that is necessary here, and understand the need to run a tight ship; and they certainly want a manager to have time to involve them, and be a 'participative' manager who is able to spend time in consultation in important areas.

So, in a nutshell:

- be clear about the rules
- apply them promptly and consistently
- when you take action, make it short and sharp
- reinforce your action, where appropriate, with systems and reminders
- remember that others are watching, and learning from, the action you take and how you take it.

Formal disciplining

The principles stated above are relevant here too. The difference is that there is a set procedure to follow. This is not the place to set out the detail of procedures influenced, certainly in the UK, by employment legislation. Suffice to say that it is necessary to work through any code in operation within your organisation (with help from any specialists available, e.g. the personnel manager). Action here tends to be progressive: a formal oral warning, a written notice, etc. Attention should be paid to the documentation, as it is possible that a clear record of events may be necessary at some future time.

Most often moving from an informal procedure to something formal is sufficient to emphasise the import of what is occurring, and once this is in train no further action may be necessary. Sometimes disciplinary action is the first move in tackling an intractable problem that can only end in dismissal (more of this later).

It is always best to be optimistic. Action needs to be selected first on the basis that common sense will prevail and behaviour will change. Only if attempts to handle the matter in a low-key way fail should more formal, and if necessary draconian, measures be taken.

➡ POOR PERFORMANCE

There are various levels of poor performance. Minor occurrences may be addressed with no more than an informal word and may be caused by something as simple as a person 'taking their eye off the ball'. Major occurrences could overlap with matters of discipline and jump you into disciplinary or dismissal procedures.

Otherwise, the progression of consideration and action is as follows:

- *Clear standards*. Such are necessary so that manager and staff know what is expected by way of performance. There is a link here back to such matters as job definition, job description and even recruitment.

- *Regular performance monitoring*. The long-term consideration here is the appraisal, but in the short term a variety of checks is possible. Without overdoing the checking-up and seeing the management role as a form of policing, controls should allow poor performance to be identified without undue delay so that consequences do not increase by default.

- *Action to change the situation.* Here, the three options of putting up with it, developing and counselling to achieve an improved capability – or firing someone – were dealt with earlier in Chapter 9. Such action needs to be decided, preferably in consultation with the poor performer, and then agreed, scheduled and seen through. Bear in mind that it might well involve a multiplicity of actions spread over some time.

- *Communication.* This is important both with the staff member concerned, and others if necessary (because poor performance might stem from something that could potentially affect others), and for the record.

The communication with someone who is presently performing poorly is clearly sensitive. On the one hand, it needs to be made clear that the situation must change, on the other, knocking confidence or rubbing noses in the dirt may make recovery more difficult.

First, it is always easier to deal with such a situation if the performance parameters are well known (and regarded as fair and reasonable). You should organise things so that it should *never* be a surprise to someone if the question of poor performance is raised. Some would go further and say that the culture should prompt people to raise problems with you or seek help before you have to take action. This is fair comment and worth thinking about.

When correction is judged possible, and once communication, which may take place over some time as attempts are made to influence results, is under way, then the following guidelines to communication style may prove useful. The intention must be to be sufficiently sensitive to prompt action without upset.

- *Focus on behaviour* rather than the person (say 'You acted too quickly' rather than 'You're an unthinking person').

- *Make observation* rather than inferences (say 'This is incomplete' rather than 'You were clearly in a rush with this').

- *Concentrate on descriptions* rather than judgements (say 'It's late' rather than 'Another example of your attitude to deadlines!').

- *Describe behaviour in a positive way* (talking about 'more' or 'less' rather than 'good' or 'bad')

- *Focus on the specific and recent* rather than abstracts from the far distance (say: 'This [specific event] happened' rather than 'You're always doing this sort of thing').

- *Sharing ideas and information* is preferable to telling (say: 'This is something others find useful that might help you' rather than 'Do it this way').

- *Explore alternatives* and different ways of doing things (asking 'How else do you think you could approach this?' rather than simply providing an alternative way as an instruction).

- *Stress the employee's commitment to the team* (saying how the person's contribution helps everyone achieve the group targets).

- *Limit the amount of information you give at any one time*, because if you overpower people with a long list of failings – even things they readily accept – some information can be lost in the volume imparted (so say: 'Let's concentrate on . . . for the moment' and keep what is said manageable, being aware that more than one session may be required).

- *Concentrate on what the employee says* rather than inferring why (say: 'If you think that . . .' rather than 'I know why you think that . . .').

None of this is designed to avoid the issue. It is more to focus on whatever may need to be sorted out in a way that will make it practical and acceptable and thus get someone really thinking about it. There may be occasions for the blunt approach, but care needs to be taken not to provoke an instant ping-pong style of argument – 'Yes you do', 'No I don't' – that leads nowhere.

Again, the precise form and style of communication can influence how a message is received and thus what action is likely to follow. There is the added bonus here that what is seen as a constructive approach is appreciated. People may know they have a problem, expect to be torn off a strip and then find that, although the point of the unacceptability of a poor performance level is strongly made, the emphasis is then on helping to correct it.

➡ DISMISSAL OF STAFF

Even firing someone is a form of communication and as such deserves a word here. The first thing to be said is that dismissal should be a rare occurrence. This is not just because for most of us it is a tasteless affair and can be difficult and embarrassing; rather, it is because it is disruptive. If selection and management are successful, they will make firing a rare occurrence.

The reasons for avoiding dismissals are similar to those that were discussed in Chapter 4 in the context of recruitment and selection, and they include the time and disruption that in that case occur as soon as it is realised that selection has been inappropriate. Here, assuming some time has passed since the employee's recruitment, additional factors may compound the difficulty. This is especially so if there is actual wrongdoing involved (e.g. theft or bullying).

If so, then this perhaps leads us to consider two categories of dismissal: automatic dismissal and failure to perform. We shall look briefly at each in turn.

With automatic dismissal, the reason for dismissal is serious and grounds for automatic ending of the person's employment. No lengthy deliberations are necessary. If someone fiddles their expenses, say, steals the petty cash or lies about a colleague to stop them being promoted, then they are likely to be dismissed. Each company must have its own clear policy about what constitutes grounds for automatic dismissal (a policy which should be openly stated). No lengthy deliberations may be necessary in terms of the manner of dismissal either. If having someone around, in disgrace and perhaps acting as a disruptive influence, is undesirable, then dismissal means leaving at once and arrangements need to be made accordingly.

With failure to perform, there does need to be more deliberation as well as a clear policy. It must be clear what constitutes 'poor' or 'inadequate' performance, and so terms of reference, performance standards and job descriptions are important – as has been said elsewhere, few things are more annoying, costly and time-consuming than facing an investigation and an industrial tribunal. With the basis for disciplinary action clear, a manager is then free to decide whether performance justifies dismissal or not. Let us look at how this is done.

Remember that, faced with inadequate performance, a manager has only three options:

1. put up with, or ignore, the problem
2. help the person to improvement and satisfactory performance
3. dismiss the person.

Number one in the list should not really be a practical option, and number two is always preferable to number three. By counselling and/or training and/or development – whatever it takes – you can work with a poor performer until that person's capabilities or willingness to deliver is brought up to standard, or you are left with just the third option.

The decision to fire is usually clear. If assistance has been tried in reasonable measure, and over a reasonable time, and yet it is clear that no improvement is going to be forthcoming, then dismissal becomes the only option. Beyond that you have to grit your teeth and do it. Bear in mind the following:

- *Check company policy and procedures.* This must be done ahead of any discussion or action (and may need to include employment legislation implications as well).

- *Early action is preferable.* Most problems of this sort do not get better of their own accord and waiting and 'hoping it will sort itself out' is not one of the options. Early action can produce the best chance of limiting damage for the organisation, and is fairer to the person being dismissed, giving them a better chance of settling successfully somewhere else.

- *Personalities can hinder action.* For the most part, people are not dismissed because they are 'bad people', only because their fit with the job is inappropriate. So beware putting off biting the bullet with people you like, if they are still inappropriate for the job in hand.

- *Communication is key.* You need to explain clearly why action is being taken and taken in a particular way (although you may want to curtail fruitless and emotional argument about it). You also need to communicate to others affected as to what is happening and why, and do so before any rumours start to fly.

- *Decisiveness is best.* While action may need to be prompt, decisive and brook no argument – 'ruthless' may even be the right word sometimes – its implementation may equally rightly be as generous as possible. Even when the reasons are clear and agreed by all, no one really likes the thought of dismissal – 'There but for the grace of God go I' – and the word goes round about it very fast. If the predominant feeling is that action was fair and settlement generous, this creates an image effect worth having. So due consideration needs to be given to notice worked and paid, pension arrangements, etc. and it may well be decided that going beyond the letter of the contract is worthwhile.

- *Documentation must be clear*. There must be no ambiguity or room for differing interpretations or argument. An accurate record of what is done, and all relevant details, must be created in writing for the person concerned, for your own records and for any central department (e.g. personnel – who may in any case sensibly be involved along the way).

It is said that you should always be nice to people on your way up an organisation as you might just meet them on the way down. The same principle applies here. The staff member whose employment is terminated may well cross paths with the company, or with you, again. If such a person at least feels (and this is more likely after a period of time rather than at the point of dismissal) that they were fairly and appropriately treated, they may not act as a lasting enemy.

Note that very similar things might be said about the process of making people *redundant*. Here, explanation and sensitivity are perhaps even more important. Similarly, the range of help that may be offered to bridge the gap and link to another job is wider and may include: counselling, practical help (by allowing use of office facilities or giving free use of an agency, for example), continuing provision of perks (such as use, or purchase on special terms, of a company car), etc. If it is possible to err on the side of generosity in terms of benefits, the effect on image and the morale of those remaining is almost always worthwhile.

As dismissal is usually the last act of communication with an employee, we shall let it conclude this chapter, albeit on a sober note. There is, however, a further positive area to review before we end.

➡ ULTIMATE CONTROL: EMPLOYEE OPINION POLLING

To be able to judge what to do, how to do it and when – and to fine-tune your communication strategy – you need to have a clear idea of what your people think. And you especially need to know about their feelings about the organisation, the management and how it affects them; indeed, you need to have a grasp of their overall motivational status. Keeping your ear to the ground and *being objective* about what you hear is important. But care is needed. Ask people questions in sensitive areas – 'What's your manager like?' – and they may tell you what they think you want to hear, or they may exaggerate their views.

Because of this difficulty, the ultimate measuring tool is the employee opinion poll. This is something that can be applied to the organisation as a whole or solely to the staff of one particular section or department. Used regularly in some organisations, such a survey can also be a useful one-off measure in times when the information it produces is particularly necessary and perhaps urgent. Examples of such circumstances include the appointment of new senior managers who have no experience of the staff, or during an organisation take-over, reorganisation or merger that creates a situation where the views of staff may be urgently needed as a preliminary to action.

The technique of employee opinion polling is, as the name suggests, a close relative of formal research techniques used to do market research or to discover political views or voting intentions. It is thus something used at a distance, as it were, and in a way that announces its intention openly. While some of the informal checking you may use as measurement does not need to be flagged specifically as checking staff motivation, this process does. It is thus best used when there is a clear reason for such a check, and when staff – though it may need explaining – will understand the reason.

Like any research, if large numbers of people are to be involved, as in a large organisation, then it is possible to take a representative sample of people rather than polling everyone. Note that what constitutes a statistically valid sample needs identifying precisely, which may be an area for expert advice, as may other aspects of the pure research techniques involved here. An excellent start to the process might be to consult the guidelines on best practice in employee research published by the [UK] Market Research Society.

Polls can be intentionally timed ahead of a change, perhaps to produce 'benchmark' information at that point; or they can be conducted after a change; or both. In all such cases, the remit may be broad. Alternatively, a poll may have a particular focus. For instance it may be useful to check employee opinions about a new development (say, a new product, or a new way of working), or about customer relations (ranging from their perception of service to technical use of a product).

As with so much else in corporate life, clear objectives are an essential ingredient of success.

Creating an environment that will allow success

The origination of a poll and the methodology it will use need careful consideration. The danger is that the very fact that a poll is being conducted will be seen as an admission of failure or difficulty, even when it is designed to prevent problems or to take an existing situation forward. Two preconditions are important to its acceptance.

The first precondition is that it is championed. This means that it is seen as being initiated by someone (who might be a functional head or even the chief executive) with a valid motive and with commitment to making it work and the clout to see it through. If it is seen as just a 'good idea', or the pet project of someone in the bowels of the personnel department, then its rationale will be more difficult to sell.

Second, the employee poll must be organised so as to make possible the gathering of genuinely open information. Opinion polls are to tell you what people *really* think. Only if people are *completely certain* that they can speak out without fear of comebacks will they do so.

The latter point means that it is virtually impossible to undertake an opinion poll, and create the necessary confidence in its confidentiality, without involving an outside agency. This may be a research company or consultancy of some sort; in any case, what is most important to staff is the perceived objectivity (and, of course, such a company's knowledge of the techniques involved may help you). Thus if a merger, say, makes polling the entire staff of an organisation necessary, involving an outsider with the resources to administer and analyse the large number of questionnaires involved may make sense. In other circumstances the task may be smaller and well within the capacities of a single consultant, so that costs need not be high.

Perhaps the most important criterion is that staff whose opinions will be sought do not see there being any vested interest lurking at the back of the project.

Communication

The methodology of the polling exercise needs to be worked out and communicated clearly. Such communication should specify the following:

- *The objective.* The reason why the poll is to be conducted should be clear, and the more specifically this is stated the better. There is a considerable difference between a project that is described as being 'just a check to see how people feel about the company', and one that is stated as being 'to provide feedback on people's current feelings, to ensure that the projected changes are carried through in a way that will enhance job satisfaction and avoid problems'. In the latter case, if there is a link to a specifically planned (and announced) change, the chances of people assisting the project are much greater.

- *The methodology.* Staff need to be told exactly how information will be collected. An assurance of confidentiality needs to be clearly given. Small details may be important – for example, if a questionnaire is to be used, how long is it and how long will it take to complete (even whether this is to be done in private time or in the firm's time may be important to some employees).

- *The reporting-back procedure.* Spell out how long this will take, who will see what, in what form and any other appropriate detail.

- *The link to action.* It should be made clear that what is being done is not producing information for information's sake, but that the results should be a route to improvements. The more that can be said about that up front, the better.

- *Any exclusions.* A poll is not a cure-all. It may help the future acceptance of findings and of actions that may follow if any areas that will *specifically not* be addressed are noted (perhaps, in some cases, how they will be addressed in other ways can be added).

- *Overall timing.* An advance announcement should spell out the full timing: when the poll will be conducted, how long it will take and when findings – and action – may be expected thereafter.

Methodology

Leaving the areas of information on one side for a moment, the canvassing of a number of staff needs to be efficiently set up and handled. The checklist shown in Box 10.1 highlights the key issues involved in ensuring the success of such an exercise.

Box 10.1 Checklist: making polling successful

The following should be borne in mind:

- Confidentiality needs to be stressed throughout the project.
- Questionnaires should be clearly anonymous and without any codes that might provide personal identification.
- Questionnaires should be quick and easy to complete (e.g. ticking boxes rather than writing essays).
- In order to double-check that a questionnaire is effective, it may be useful to 'pilot' it – i.e. to use it first on a limited basis to test it.
- Questions should be carefully worded and unambiguous.*
- Providing information should be strictly voluntary (though all the communication about the project should be such as to persuade most people to *want* to participate).
- Any unions or staff organisations should be consulted and kept informed, and this is best started at an early stage.
- Time to complete the questionnaire should be provided (i.e. rather than requesting it back 'at the end of the week' or whatever, it may be better to pull people away from work and give them a set time to complete the information).
- A ballot-box type of collection process may be useful to emphasise confidentiality.
- Resources must be in place to see the project through and do so on time, because nothing creates a lack of credibility faster than saying that views will be canvassed, and that they will influence action, and then nothing happens – or nothing happens for a long time.
- Consider using other communication methods alongside the

project communication to reinforce the impact (e.g. an internal newsletter or company magazine could report progress to date or give out certain advance findings).

NOTE: Care should also be taken to make sure that questions do not act in a leading manner. For example, to take a general example, if a political pollster asked: 'Would you pay more in tax if this guaranteed less congestion on the roads?', this would perhaps prompt a different answer from the question: 'How important would you rate the need to reduce the congestion on the roads?' Similarly, if a question incorporates an opinion ('Annual job appraisals are very important, do you agree: very strongly, strongly, etc.') rather than positioning its content without any prejudgement ('How highly would you rate annual job appraisals, etc?'), then the latter is surely more likely to produce useful, rather than biased, information.

The areas of questioning

There can be no universal standard questionnaire. Questioning must reflect the organisation and the jobs and responsibilities of those polled. In a particular organisation it may be possible to use one questionnaire to get a general idea of feelings around the whole workforce. However, if the polling is focused on one category of staff, or even one department, then more specific questions are possible, and more tailoring of the format will be necessary.

Rating scales used in a poll questionnaire can be made most pointed when respondents are asked to select from an *even* number of options. This removes the option of a middle point – the ubiquitous average – and tends to produce more action-oriented information. If the intention is indeed to provide a basis for action, then this is surely better. Thus questions might ask respondents to tick whether something happens: never: seldom: usually: always; or whether something is regarded as being: very useful: quite useful: not very useful: useless. And so on, depending on the topic of the question.

The example shown in Box 10.2 gives a checklist of information that is the first stage to preparing a tailor-made questionnaire.

Box 10.2 Checklist: compiling a poll questionnaire

The following takes as an example one specific category of staff – in this case members of a field sales team – to show how question areas can be selected for an employee opinion poll, and how specific questions can focus on the particulars of the role and tasks involved.

Question areas might include the following (shown with some examples of the detailed areas that might be explored within each).

The product range sold

How easy are the products to sell?

How are they rated by customers?

How are they positioned alongside competitive products (or services)?

The customers dealt with

What is customers' attitude to the organisation and to the sales team?

How do customers rate the service they receive?

What would make our customers increase business with us?

Support provided

Are requests for support (on behalf of customers) promptly and efficiently dealt with?

Is information, and sales aids, provided by the organisation relevant and useful?

Are the sales meetings held constructive and useful?

Relationships with others around the organisation

How are relationships with other departments (e.g. technical or marketing) rated?

Are communications channels with others internally satisfactory?

Does action taken by others strengthen the sales relationship with customers?

Career opportunities

Do people see career opportunities as a reason to stay with the organisation?

Are longer-term career issues discussed?
How does this organisation seem to rate against other potential employers?

Supervision
How is the respondent's immediate line manager rated (as someone to work for)?
Are objectives clearly spelt out and targets set sensibly and fairly?
Are contact and communications with the supervisor satisfactory and supportive?

Rewards
What are attitudes to salary?
How is the total package regarded (including incentives linked to performance)?
What changes would be appreciated?

Team working
How effectively does the team work together?
Does competition within the team help or hinder the achievement of planned results?
Are there any areas that give rise to friction amongst the group?

Work conditions
Are travel or time away from home intrusive or unreasonable?
What attitude is there to the required reporting systems?
Are there particular factors (e.g. company cars) about which there are suggestions or complaints?

Training and development
Do you feel the right training is provided and is there sufficient of it?
Are there fears for the future about skills falling behind the needs of the market?
Do you see your job as something repetitive or as something that expands in scope over time?

Personal details

As questionnaires are anonymous it may be useful to collect some basic personal information to help position and analyse the answers given.

What age bracket are you in?
How long have you worked for the company?
Are you male or female?

Follow-up interviews

Findings from an employee poll may be taken further in order to explore issues in depth or more widely by using individual interviews. People must be selected carefully for this. A sample of the full group of employees being canvassed may be chosen, and this might be done at random (taking perhaps 10–15 per cent of the total group being canvassed). Alternatively, the full group from the poll can be used to identify the subgroup required for individual interview.

This would be achieved by asking – perhaps as one of the questionnaire questions – for nominations of people who the respondent feels will give a representative view on behalf of a group of employees. Then either individuals can be chosen at random from those who have been nominated, or a weighting factor can be introduced, for instance by asking for several nominations and then selecting those whose names crop up most frequently.

It should be noted that this aspect of the poll should, like the rest, be voluntary. Some so selected may opt not to go for interview. The fact that the objectives have been clearly explained and that the interviewer is not a member of the organisation's management will help ensure this is minimal.

Analysis of the interview results should also be conducted promptly (at worst, long delays will be interpreted as doctoring the findings). And the findings need to be published in full; if necessary this means 'warts and all'. Omitting any aspect of the coverage of questions asked is dangerous. Employees will always put the worst interpretation on why answers to certain questions are not included (thus probably exaggerating any problem).

Often, the categories of staff involved are not familiar with reports setting out a mass of figures, and so it is useful to make sure that the presentation of the findings is easy to read. The answers to main questions, most often selecting some form of rating, can best be set out in graphical form – for example as a pie chart – and this should help to make easily digestible the proportions of employees who think what.

And in summary . . .

While not every organisation will want to undertake something so extensive or formal as an employee opinion poll, such polls are useful. One focus worth investigating is certainly communication: gaining accurate information on exactly what people think of the culture and practice of the organisation and its management with regard to the communications directed at them. Even small versions of this sort of approach can be useful and, whatever else, it should be borne in mind that feedback is vital and that it must be as objective as possible. After all, your next piece of communication must be based on a good, clear and up-to-date picture of the people you must communicate with and how they feel.

With all such matters, the individual is constrained or helped by what goes on around them. Other people, policy and practice all tend to make what the individual wants to do either easier or more difficult. Like so much else, this is not simply a 'given'; the culture itself can be influenced and made more positive in its effect. It is to this we turn next.

Chapter 11
A culture of communication

A wise man will make more opportunities than he finds.

(Francis Bacon)

The power of an organisation's culture is considerable. 'Culture' in this sense is perhaps best defined as a combination of perceived best practice – 'the way we do things round here' – and commitment. Although difficult to define, it is something we all know when we meet it. Corporate culture, which can easily be interpreted as the prevailing atmosphere at department level as well as more widely, is partly unspecific – it manifests itself as 'good feelings' in various ways. But it is also very specific.

For example, I can still remember being amazed by one particular aspect of the culture in the first consultancy firm I joined. It seemed anyone could walk into anyone else's office and ask for help; and they always received it. People might not drop everything and say, 'Sit down' instantly. They did, however, always offer something – 'Can you come back in half an hour?', 'How about getting together this afternoon?' For a newcomer, tackling new things and feeling his way in the firm, this was a godsend. I discovered that this attitude was encouraged – actively fostered – by management (especially a few individuals), but that it was maintained not in any sense to conform, but just because it worked. Everyone in the firm benefited. Two heads are better than one, and it was a business in which consultation, transfer of experience and flushing out new creative approaches were all essential. No one seemed to find themselves taking an unrestricted or unreasonable burden of such sessions. Everyone was involved, and the load was shared. This is a clear example of the power of culture within an organisation –

something being achieved not because of an instruction or system but because of a common belief.

That said, exactly *how* such belief is instilled is less clear. But it is possible, so we need to consider how it might be achieved.

➡ SETTING THE CULTURAL SCENE

The first thing that needs to be said is that culture generation needs commitment from the top. This may imply the chief executive, or simply the head of a department on a more 'local' scale. It is possible for useful practices to be initiated at grass-roots level, of course, but it is difficult for them to stick and spread without support.

Usually the rationale is practical. In the example above, it was the nature of the work that made working together so useful: brief, practical, mutual help-sessions evolved because they were useful. Similarly, a company may develop a strong feeling for customer service that stems primarily from a common sense analysis of what is necessary, in a competitive world, to win and sustain business. So the starting point to creating an appropriate culture is an analysis of what needs to be achieved, and then what sort of behaviour is likely to assist the process.

When useful cultural behaviour begins to occur, it will be sustained better if it applies to everyone. Senior and less senior staff alike need to be involved (as was very much the case in my consultancy example). The behaviour of the senior people can then act like a role model for others. Their being seen to participate characterises the nature of the behaviour. It does not become 'something we are being asked (or told) to do'; rather, it is seen as something that most people seem to find desirable – and that works. At this point word of mouth becomes an important way of sustaining the impetus of the cultural change.

Beyond this, formal systems may have a role to play and managers may want to look for ways to maintain or increase awareness of an aspect of the culture – for example, through items in company newsletters or on notice boards.

No secrets

One factor ranks high as a potential dampener of useful cultural behaviour and that is secrecy – or, rather, unnecessary secrecy. Now let us be clear here: some facts need, at particular moments, to be kept confidential. And a balance is necessary, simply because telling everyone everything that goes on in a large organisation would be prohibitively time-consuming. That said, feeling that things – especially things that might affect them – are being kept from people for no good reason (or for patronising reasons – 'They wouldn't understand') annoys and antagonises. It creates a culture of unease and wariness. It makes co-operation seem undesirable and hinders the build-up of any behaviour or belief that may be being encouraged.

The moral is simple: think carefully before you decide that 'no one needs to know'. Think about the timing, and build in a systematic element of keeping people involved and up-to-date. Many developments are good. People will not only like to know about them, but they may also be able to help, support or simply sing the praises of what is to happen.

This does not apply to everything, of course. Some developments are bad. Some will affect people adversely. Even so, a news bombshell that upsets staff will make it very difficult to carry people with you or to muster their support or co-operation. Staff will resent not being informed. They will feel belittled in their importance, and they will react accordingly.

As a result, many projects should prompt thinking about the communications aspect of their planning. You must think through and decide:

- who should be informed
- when people should be informed
- how often they should be updated on progress or developments
- what feedback mechanisms need to be in place.

Above all, you as a manager need to be sure that such communication makes it very clear *why* things are being done, and done in the way they are. Conflict (see Chapter 10) may need nipping in the bud.

In contrast, an open attitude – one that staff appreciate because it respects them – actively builds goodwill and collaboration. In many organisations there is resentment about secrets that have no real need to be secrets; in such circumstances, a little more communication can change beliefs and behaviour.

As a (perhaps extreme) example of open management, I can mention that I know more than one organisation where all salaries are public knowledge. Anyone can walk into the chief accountant's office and ask what someone else is paid. No harm seems to be done. The greatest impact is on those responsible for deciding the level of salaries. It means that all differentials – how one person's salary relates to another – must be rationally explicable. And that seem wholly right. The net result is that people *expect* all differentials to be fair. Attention to the policy means that they are, in which case what is there to hide? Now, let me be clear: I am *not* suggesting that this would necessarily be right for every organisation. Yet it does certainly demonstrate that there may be many areas where reflexes dictate secrecy, yet where this is not actually important and where increased openness might well add something to the prevailing culture.

➡ COMMUNICATION SYSTEMS

The role of a variety of systems can be turned to act in support of the communication culture you want. The following are examples, and you may well be able to think of more. Consider:

- *meetings*: staff meetings, project meetings, even company-wide conferences can all have an element that builds the culture – reporting successes, looking ahead, etc.
- *newsletters*: any regular missive can be part of what is done (and this includes such devices as notice boards and such methods as e-mail)
- *suggestion schemes*: often much maligned, these can be a very useful spur to employee involvement, provided that there is good feedback and that credit (and perhaps reward) is given appropriately and fairly
- *quality circles*: the (Japanese-originated) system of meetings and exchanges designed to improve quality can in fact be focused on any specific topic (e.g. customer care procedures) and can be made to be seen as a useful – and regular – element of communications
- *planning*: the preparation of many plans, including at some levels

the business or marketing plan, should be linked to consultation and inputs from a variety of levels

- *change management*: for organisations going through noticeable or important change, there may need to be regular ongoing communication focusing on just that

- *social activities*: these too play a part, and gatherings can be designed to achieve specific purpose (e.g. the combining of two departments) provided that the social element does not suffer and the purpose is not seen as contrived.

➡ ACCENTUATE THE POSITIVE

In all communication there is a need to focus on the positive. There are always two ways of looking at everything. It is important that a message comes over in a way that increases optimism and prompts the action or support that circumstances make necessary. For example, something like a move to new premises may spark dread: the upheaval, the backlog of work, the worry about 'my new location' and uncertainties about conditions and facilities. The communication can counter this by focusing on the positive: an opportunity to reorganise, an improved image, better conditions of work for people, how the plan will minimise difficulties, and the underlying reason why it is necessary (which might be growth, success or an opportunity to expand further in future).

No one wants to work for a manager who is all doom and gloom, especially as such an attitude may prove contagious and create a culture of 'seeing problems everywhere'. As a manager you need to develop a firm habit of thinking before you speak in this respect, analysing both sides of any situation and putting problems in perspective by stressing the positive side and the positive results to be aimed for through the exercise.

➡ EMPOWERMENT

Early on, the point was made that telling people what to do is no longer a main element of management. Teams of people are most powerful when they have a reasonable degree of self-sufficiency. Sometimes controls and the need for tight supervision are perpetuated only because there is an assumption that they are necessary.

Times and circumstances change, so that even something that was once absolutely necessary does not necessarily continue for ever.

I remember analysing a situation in a company that I had as a client some years ago. A particular decision with regard to customers (it linked to product exchange-and-return, but the details are not important here) always had to be checked with a supervisor. This took time (which costs money) and reduced the speed of customer service as staff went to and fro to find and discuss the matter with their supervisor. But management felt that their input was important. So we monitored separately the decisions the supervisors made alongside those the staff said they would make if allowed to do so. The views of what action should be taken were almost always identical. In other words the delay, the check and the consultation did not affect the action. The check was discontinued, and customer service thereby improved. So too did motivation, of course, as people felt trusted and liked taking responsibility by trusting their own judgement.

Such situations are not uncommon. You need to think about the attitude you take to giving people their head and letting them take responsibility for their own actions. Setting up how things will work, briefing people and, if necessary, giving them the authority and the knowledge to act alone is necessary first, but a manager should surely aim at a high level of self-sufficiency amongst the team wherever possible.

➡ SUMMARY OF THE CHAPTER

Everything that has been discussed in these pages is easier for the individual manager to achieve when there is a culture in the organisation that is supportive of good staff communications. In fact, culture goes further than this. It initiates and maintains action and fosters ongoing attitudes and work habits that make efficiency and effectiveness more likely.

This is not something that you can afford to only respond to. There will be influences at work in your organisation that will create some sort of corporate culture unless you and your colleagues do. So the only question is what will be the dominant influence and what will be the nature of the culture thus created. Managers have a responsibility to influence the culture – indeed, to consider what it should comprise and to actively aim to create what is most helpful.

If the lead in establishing the culture of the organisation comes from the top, so much the better. If not, you and others may need to take an initiative in creating and maintaining a culture, and perhaps also encouraging senior management to play its part. This latter may be a longer-term educational process, given the intransigence of some senior managers.

One thing is certain: culture affects results, and in the area under discussion the communication culture affects your ability to make your communications work as well as you wish. If you are not actively involved in culture creation, you are leaving something important to chance or allowing it to go by default. A little action here may make a considerable difference.

Afterword

The real leader has no need to lead – he is content to point the way.

(Henry Miller)

There are two factors that I would like to touch on briefly by way of summary in the last pages of this book. The first concerns the commitment that a manager must have towards their staff communication. The benefits have been spelt out throughout this book; but they do not just fall into your lap. That should be clear too.

➡ A POSITIVE COMMITMENT

Communication is itself inherently difficult. Every day, examples of potential problems accumulate, creating either nonsense or confusion or both. Maximising the effectiveness of communication inevitably takes time. Sometimes a moment's thought is all that is necessary; sometimes longer consideration, consultation and planning is necessary. Yet the most productive and effective manager I have ever known is also the best example I know of someone who practises good staff communications.

How is making time for this possible? First, the person concerned is committed to the necessity of good staff communication. By taking time and working at it, he fits it in, gets it right and reaps the benefits. His team is exceptionally self-sufficient. He spends little time fighting fires or picking up pieces. And when he does, he does so in a way that is designed not only to sort out any immediate problem but also to minimise the likelihood of something similar causing problems in the future. There is a virtuous circle at work here. By spending the time and getting communications right, he ensures better performance from his team, which in turn is a prime factor in his being able to give sufficient time to communications.

This is not simply a demonstration of the need for commitment to the communications process, however. It reflects also his conviction that getting the process right is a significant contributor to creating positive motivation. His communication is a significant part of the motivating he undertakes, and this makes both processes more productive. The results build on each other and the net result is a strong team that performs well.

➡ MAXIMISING THE OPPORTUNITY

A second factor is also prime. Just implementing the communication that is dictated by operational activity is insufficient to maximise the effect: you have, rather, to actively seek opportunities to *create* communication opportunities and make them work hard. Much of what is useful in this respect is simply a case of going a little further than is necessary. The general manager, referred to in Chapter 7 in the context of training, who took the time not only to introduce a training event but also to host a get-together afterwards, was creating an opportunity for useful staff communication. He added noticeably to the effectiveness of the situation. It took a moment to think through and a little time to execute, but not too much; and he continued doing it only because experience seemed to indicate that it was worthwhile to do so.

As well as creating opportunities in this way, you as a manager need to maximise the usefulness of even routine communications situations. An example that sticks in my memory from way back will serve to illustrate. Very early in my career I was appointed for the first time to a small management committee – a small but significant step in my career progression (I hoped!). I was (albeit for what I thought were good reasons) a minute or two late for my first meeting of the group, and I arrived to find the room locked and no one answering my knocks. I returned to my desk wondering what to make of this and raised it with my boss later in the day, asking what had happened and, with the conference room locked, where the meeting had been held. He simply looked me in the eye and asked: 'What time did you arrive?'

He had locked the door! There were all sorts of things he could have done – for example, allowing me to slip in and telling me later how important it was to be punctual. But by choosing a more dramatic way, he minimised the time the subsequent discussion needed and made a much more powerful point. I was never late for one of his meetings again; nor, for the most part, was anyone else. He ran a tight ship. I learnt a great deal from him (including a healthy regard for the virtue of being punctual!) and this kind of gesture was always done in a friendly and constructive way.

That manager was a master at maximising the effectiveness of any communication with his team, and he was a popular and effective manager at the same time – one who also maximised the motivational impact of everything he did. These days the pace, rush and stress of organisational life is considerable. Thinking of and carrying out communication in a way that achieves this much is not easy, and the IT revolution makes it somehow more difficult. An e-mail, for instance, is characterised by its brevity and informality – and very often by its short life; it flashes on the screen, is noted, and then, at the push of a button, is gone for ever. Making a message make a real point, and making that point linger in the memory, is a real challenge.

The opportunity presented to you here is considerable. Some managers allow poor staff communications to dilute their effectiveness (and if this is the case, it is as likely to be caused by unthinking action as wrong action). Some managers are good and clear with the staff communication that is necessary.

And others go further. They see the opportunity. They commit to taking advantage of it. They work at the detail in order to squeeze every possible advantage out of every situation. There is no doubt which kind of manager staff prefer; or which achieve most. The choice is yours.

Patrick Forsyth
Touchstone Training and Consultancy
28 Saltcote Maltings
Heybridge
Maldon
Essex CM9 4QP

Index